M O N E Y

...and how it multiplies!

A Practical Guide for
Effective Money Management

Dr. Mia Y. Merritt

ISBN #978-0-9835830-9-7

Other Books by Mia Y. Merritt:
Prosperity is Your Birthright!
Prosperity is Your Birthright Workbook
Destined for Great Things!
Destined for Great Things Workbook
Words of Inspiration
Life After High School
Life After High School Workbook
The Road the Inner Joy & Peace
Releasing Emotional Baggage

Library of Congress Cataloging
in-Publication Data

Merritt, Mia

First Printing 2012
Printed in the U.S.A.

INTRODUCTION

Understanding how money works is the first step toward making it work for you. Let's face it, everybody wants a lot of money because money makes the world go round and buys a lot of awesome stuff! People who have a lot of it are respected, esteemed and envied. From the time you reached the age of understanding money, you wanted it and the desire for it has not diminished. You still want it. The majority of what people do is for money because money solves many problems, although not all. For instance, people go to college so they can earn the credentials to get a good job that makes a lot of MONEY. Some go into the military so they can get MONEY to pay for college. People play the lottery in order to win MONEY. People work overtime for more MONEY. Money seems to be the primary motive for many things that people do. And that is just fine as long as you spend it wisely and make strategic investments. The purpose of this book is to teach you the fundamental principles of financial management. The main thing that you really need to remember is that it is not how much money you make that counts, it is how much you save. It is not the size of your income that will determine your financial well-being over the next 20 to 30 years, it is how you invest the money you make.

Contents

How Money Works

Money is like a sixth sense - and you can't make use
of the other five without it.

~William Somerset Maugham

The way you handle your money will impact almost every financial aspect of your life, from your personal education to the education of your children, the kind of car and home you buy, and the type of contribution you will make to your community. There is a secret to making money work for you and if you learn the secrets now, you will be financially better off in the future. Now is the time to learn those secrets and now is the time to make the sacrifices that will give you financial freedom. If you start applying the secrets while you are young, you will reap the benefits when you get older and you will be very happy you did. The average person spends money as they wish. As soon as the money comes in, it goes right back out and a cycle of living from paycheck to paycheck is perpetuated. There is no financial plan, no spending strategy and no extra money available in case of emergencies. Because of this haphazard and frivolous spending, a large amount of debt is eventually created along with a bad Credit Report, repossessions, evictions, foreclosures and bankruptcies. It could take years to get your financial credibility back on the right track. If you spend more than you make, you will always be in debt, always stressed, rarely happy and eventually poor or bankrupt. Many new college graduates find that in the first couple years of working, they have excess cash flow and are making more money than they ever dreamed of, thanks to that college degree. They usually use that extra cash on buying new clothes, a sporty car or the latest electronic devices. However, this excess money could or should be put towards reducing debt, not creating it, adding to their savings account, emergency fund or retirement account. There will be plenty of time to buy the toys.

Managing money is an area that requires discipline, and the sooner you learn how to appropriately handle your money, the more financially secure you will be. Unfortunately, personal finance was not a required subject in high school or college and as a result, if you have not been blessed enough to have someone sit you down and talk to you about smart money matters, you might be oblivious as to how to strategically manage it and make it grow; but the smarter you are about your money, the better off you will be in terms of spending, saving, and investing. You must make it an automatic habit of saving a portion of every dollar you earn. No matter how large your paycheck is, if you do not save, you will never live a life of financial abundance. Let's start with the basics:

GET A "FREE" CHECKING & SAVINGS ACCOUNT

The first smart thing to do is find a bank that offers free checking and savings accounts. If you already have a checking and savings account and are paying a monthly fee, call your bank and see if you can switch to a free account. Some banks will offer a free checking account provided you keep a minimum amount in the account. This is not the one I am talking about. Inquire about the "free" account. This is one small way to save money each month, because with a free account, you do not have the monthly fee regardless of how small that fee is. Ten dollars a month totals $120.00 a year. That is money that could be earning interest in your savings account or placed in your Emergency Fund. Also make sure that with your free accounts, you have access to online banking and online bill pay. Additionally, if the bank offers free standard checks, take advantage of these as well. Why pay more money for customized checks when the plain ones do the same things as the customized ones? Moreover, be sure to get the duplicate checks. That way, you have a copy of every check that you write. If you write a large number of checks, it may be to your advantage to shop around for the best price. Some banks charge up to $25 for a box of 200 checks. You can get that same box much cheaper by ordering directly from the printer. *Checks in the Mail* (800-733-4443) and *Checks Unlimited* (800-210-0468) offer checks at a significantly discounted price and they offer a wider range of designs than many of the banks do.

As you write checks, make sure that you keep your checkbook balanced to ensure that the money to cover each check written is available. Check your bank account frequently online in order to make sure that you are not running low on funds and that you have no overdrafts. Overdraft fees add up quickly and deplete your funds. You also want to check your account frequently to make sure that no unauthorized withdrawals have been made. Identify theft has become all too common these days.

REVIEW YOUR MONTHLY INCOME

This is the beginning of budgeting and the start to becoming financially responsible. Look at the amount of money you bring home each month (your net income) and compare that figure to the amount that you spend each month. Ideally, the income should be larger than the output. If this is not the case, then some stringent changes must be made. If you are spending more than you are earning, it is time to review your spending habits. When the expenditures are larger than the income, you have one only option: cut your expenses. Otherwise, your expenses will become so overwhelming that you can no longer afford to pay them all on time. Things begin to get paid late and then you have a credit problem. Keep in mind that you always want to strive for a good Credit Score.

BENEFITS OF HAVING GOOD CREDIT

Credit is a privilege, not a right! Having good credit puts you head and shoulders above those with bad credit. A high credit rating shows that you have been responsible with credit that was given to you in the past and can be trusted to pay back what is loaned to you in the future. This means that lenders will be more likely to loan you money, offer you larger lines of credit and give you a lower interest rate. Having good credit is the key to getting the most out of your money because it means that less of your money goes towards paying high interest rates and more goes towards paying off the principle balance of your loan. Paying back your debts in a timely manner helps you to maintain a good credit history and will allow you to get better rates on major purchases.

It is very wise to check your Credit Report every six to twelve months and at least three months before making a major purchase. This will give you the heads up on any erroneous entries on your report and will prevent you from being blindsided by things that you didn't even know was on your report. Checking your Credit Report frequently can also protect you against identity theft. Paying your bills on time, keeping your credit card balances low (below 35%), and correcting any negative mistakes on the report all contribute to maintaining a healthy credit profile.

THINGS TO DO TO KEEP YOUR CREDIT IN GOOD STANDING:

1. PAY ALL YOUR BILLS ON TIME.

This is the main thing that lenders look for when they consider extending credit to you. When your statements come, they will have a due date and a recommended mail date. Always get your payment in before the due date. Late payments will not only adversely affect your Credit Report, but a late fee will be assessed and it is usually pretty hefty.

2. ALWAYS PAY THE MINIMUM PAYMENT DUE.

If you pay less than the minimum payment due, it is just as bad as having a late payment and will be reported on your credit as late because the minimum payment was not received. It is fine to pay more than the minimum due, but never pay less.

3. PAY EXTRA ON THE MINIMUM PAYMENT.

Even if you only pay five dollars on top of what is due, it looks good on your report and shows that you are making an effort to pay back what is owed quicker than scheduled. Paying more than the minimum also contributes to you paying lesser interest fees because as you pay more on the principal balance, you pay less in interest.

4. ALWAYS KEEP A BALANCE.

I know that you might think that paying accounts in full will make your credit score increase, but the truth is that you should always leave a little balance on each card because each month that you make an on-time payment, it looks very good for you. However, if you pay an account balance completely off, it does increase your credit score because your debt amount goes down, but it stops right there, whereas if you are always making on-time payments, it shows that you are consistent and reliable.

5. DON'T MAX OUT YOUR CREDIT CARDS OR GO OVER YOUR LIMIT.

This is a big "no no" because when you max out your credit cards and/or go over the limit, it looks like you are not managing your money well. You will also have to pay those hefty over-the-limit fees that are added to the principal balance.

6. MINIMIZE OUTSTANDING DEBT.

Try and pay at least 50% of large debts. The less debt you have, the better. If you can not do this, then at least try and get your credit card bills down to 50% of what is owed or less.

7. REFRAIN FROM APPLYING FOR CREDIT UNNECESSARILY.

Sometimes when you go shopping, they may ask you to apply for a credit card and get 10 or 20 percent off your purchase right then and there if you are instantly approved. Politely say no. Pay the price for what you are buying and walk away. If you do not need another credit card, then do not apply for another one.

8. KEEP OLD ACCOUNTS OPEN.

Keep in mind that old accounts that are open and paid on time are very good. Creditors look for accounts open for more than seven years and in good standing. Do not close these accounts. They work in your favor.

9. REVIEW YOUR CREDIT REPORT FREQUENTLY.

This is a smart and wise thing to do. Remember that you should review your Credit Report every six months, but minimally every year. You need to know what is on there and who is pulling and reviewing your information. You also need to make sure that information on you is accurate and up to date.

10. GO AUTOMATIC.

Setting up an automatic payment plan with your credit card companies and lenders can help ensure that you never miss your minimum payment due, but make sure the money is in the account on the day of the withdrawal! Online bill pay has proven to work well for people.

Some people do not realize how important it really is to build good credit until they have allowed their credit score to plummet. Learn the steps you can take in order to build and keep good credit. If you have allowed your credit to go bad, you can still build it back up again. Don't get discouraged. Even bad credit ratings can be improved and fixed. Depending on the situation, with responsible credit usage and prompt payments, bad credit can turn into good credit over time.

FINANCIAL TIPS TO REMEMBER:

- ✓ You must make it an automatic habit of saving a portion of every dollar you earn.

- ✓ As you write checks, make sure that you keep your checkbook balanced to ensure that the money to cover each check written is available.

- ✓ If you are spending more than you are earning, it is time to review your spending habits. When the expenditures are larger than the income, you have one only option: cut your expenses.

- ✓ Paying back your debts in a timely manner helps you to maintain a good credit history and will allow you to get better rates on major purchases.

- ✓ If you have allowed your credit to go bad, you can still build it back up again. Don't get discouraged.

Create your Spending Plan

Too many people spend money they haven't earned, to buy things they don't want, to impress people they don't like.

~Will Smith

When we hear the words "fixed income", we immediately think of the elderly whose only income may be a small social security or retirement check, but the truth is that we all are on a "fixed income". Whatever salary we make, determines what we can and can not afford to have. Working towards financial freedom does not have to be an exercise in self-deprivation, as many people think. Even the wealthy are on a "fixed income". If they have an income of two million a year, then they have to live within the confines of what that money allows (however, they may have some extra incentives based upon their credit worthiness). You must know what your money allows you to do and intelligently allocate that money within the confines of that limit. Spending money that you do not have can become incredibly expensive, especially if you do not have the money to pay it back. Sticking to a Spending Plan (budget) can curtail all of this. Once you get into the habit of being financially disciplined, you will begin to reap the financial benefits.

There are spreadsheets and software programs designed to make the budgeting process faster and easier, but essentially, all you really need is a piece of paper, a pencil, and the desire to live within (or even below) your means for now. When creating a Spending Plan, the main things to take into account are rent/mortgage, car payment, insurance(s), utilities, food and credit card bills. Everything else is secondary. The key to getting out of debt efficiently is to pay down the balances of loans or credit cards that have the highest interest rate while paying at least the minimum due on all your other debt. Once the high-interest debt is paid down, then tackle the next highest, and so on.

BUILD YOUR EMERGENCY FUND

An Emergency Fund is a necessity. Someday you will definitely need it. To quote the American poet Henry Wadsworth Longfellow, *"Into each life some rain must fall. Some days must be dark and dreary."* You must have some money saved for when that rainy day comes. Like every other recurring item in your budget, the emergency fund is something you put money into each month until you reach your desired goal. Financial experts recommend to save a cash reserve large enough to cover three to six month's worth of monthly expenses. If you lose your job, your bills must still be paid and it may take a few months to find another suitable job, but with an Emergency Fund, you do not have to panic right away, because the money in the fund will sustain you for a while. In life you must expect the unexpected, and this is why you need an Emergency Fund. The main purpose of this particular fund is in the case of loss of employment. However, other major expenses may arise as in unexpected medical expenses, major home or car repairs or some other unexpected expense that requires a lot of money to be spent. It is best to plan for a worst-case scenario so that the smaller emergencies such as replacing the water heater that just died can be easily covered.

If you currently do not have an Emergency Fund or find it difficult to save, the key is to start small. Even if you only start with $10.00 in the beginning, at least you have taken the initiative to start. The main thing is to be consistent in adding to your Emergency Fund until you can gradually increase the amount you put in it. Other than your health, your income is probably your most important asset. Lose it and you could be losing your primary means of financial security. That is why every working adult needs an Emergency Fund. It will not be built over night. Accumulating one month's worth of expenses will take some time and requires disciplined effort to achieve. Saving three to six months worth of expenses is no easy task. However, if you set your immediate goals to be small and manageable, you will have a better chance in reaching those goals eventually. The best way to get started is through automatic withdrawal. The next step is to set up regular withdrawal amounts into this account. Whether it is weekly, bi-weekly or monthly, create a schedule and stick to it. Eventually, you won't even miss the money you put into this fund. Having money in savings to use for emergencies can really keep you out of trouble financially and help you sleep better at night. Also, if you get into the habit of saving money and treating that money as a non-negotiable monthly expense, pretty soon you will have more than just emergency money saved up. You will eventually have vacation money, retirement money, and even money for a nice down payment on a new home. Take a look below of the example provided. I have listed the monthly expenses for a modest household. Let's see how much should go into the Emergency Fund for this household:

MONTHLY EXPENSES:

Rent/Mortgage	$900
Electricity	$175
Car Payment	$520
Car Insurance	$140
Utilities	$150
Groceries	$150
Credit Cards	$300
Internet	$60
Cell Phone	$89
Miscellaneous	$200
Total Monthly Expenses	**$2,684**

EMERGENCY FUND AMOUNT:

1 Month	$2,684
2 Months	$5,368
3 Months	**$8,052**
4 Months	$10,736
5 Months	$13,420
6 Months	**$16,104**

If this illustration was *your* household, you would need a minimum of $8,052 (3 months) and a maximum of $16,104 (6 months) in your Emergency Fund. At first glance it may seem like a lot of money, but it really is realistic to accomplish. Also keep in mind that the above illustration is for a "modest" household. Most people's bills are much more than what is indicated there. Consistency in putting money in and NOT TOUCHING THAT MONEY is the secret. Let it automatically be withdrawn out of your bank account and do NOT have a debit card for this account if you can help it. The great pyramids were built one brick at a time. An alcoholic became a drunk by one drink at a time. A long drive is made one mile at a time and your Emergency Fund will become substantial one dollar at a time (well maybe $10.00 or $20.00 but you get my point).

In order to reach your targeted goals, you must have a plan and execute it. The first step is to determine how much you spend each month. If you spend more than you bring in, then it is time to curtail your spending by cutting out some things. Once you do this, you must factor in how much you can afford to put into your Emergency Fund and how long it will take to reach your one month goal, two month goal, etc. View your emergency fund as an insurance policy and guard it carefully. Do not dip into it for incidental expenses. Use it only for the purpose in which it was intended – for emergencies, and pray that an emergency never happens. Remember, once that money is spent, it takes some time to replenish it. Start now and save whatever you can, even if it is not that much. You will be glad you did!

LEARN SELF CONTROL!

What keeps most people living from paycheck to paycheck is that they are always spending money on stuff they do not need. From experience, I can tell you that the younger most people are, the harder it is to exercise self-control when it comes to money, because when they see something they want and there is a way to get it, young people will usually get it. That's just a fact, but what is sadder is that many older people still have no self-control and they will get something they see and then have to struggle to pay their bills later. However, the sooner you learn the fine art of delaying gratification, the sooner you will find that it is easy to keep your finances in order. Keeping your recurring monthly expenses as low as possible will also save you big bucks over time. Although it seems relatively easy to purchase an item on your credit card the minute you see it, it is better to wait until you have the cash for it. Think about it, do you really want to pay interest on a new leather jacket or a box of cereal? It is not smart to use credit cards for things that you consume quickly or are non-essential, such as meals, groceries or clothes or shoes. If you can not afford to pay off what you put on that card in one or two months, then try not to use the card and avoid paying substantial interest charges. There is no faster way to fall into debt than haphazardly using credit cards. Instead of using your credit card for non-essential things, put aside some cash each month for those items, so you can pay for it in full when the time comes. It has taken me some years to develop self-discipline in this area, so now when I see something I think I want, I ask myself the following questions:

1. Are all my bills paid up?
2. Have I reached my Emergency Fund Goal?
3. Can I live without this and do I really need it?
4. What is the real reason I want it?

This is how I keep myself level-headed. If the answers to the first two questions are "no" I leave the item right where it is. You will get to this point too. You absolutely must begin to practice self-control when shopping and learn to walk away from things. Do you really need that 85 dollar pair of shoes? What else can be done with that $85 dollars that you want to spend on those shoes? If you put those shoes on a credit card, you may just be paying for those same shoes two years from now. Where many people get into trouble is that they feel entitled to a standard of living that exceeds what they can afford. However, if you keep your standard of living *below* what you earn, you will not have to cut back to save money, instead, you will have excess cash flow because you will earn more than you need to live on. Keep in mind that when you try to keep up with the Joneses, you are setting your personal finances up for disaster. If you manage your money right, the Jones family will eventually be trying to keep up with you.

Although it is beneficial to know what to do in order to live within your means and maintain good credit, it is equally important to know what not to do. If you have read this far in this book, then you are to be commended! The challenge is to take the information that you have learned and seriously apply it into your life. Completing the activities in the *Life After High School Workbook* will help you to remember this valuable information. You will be many steps ahead of the game if you apply the strategies necessary to build and maintain good credit. Things that make a good Credit Report and earn you high credit scores are essential to know, but things that make a poor report and lowers your credit score are also important to know. Therefore, I have identified for you below a list of things to avoid doing in order to keep your credit in good standing:

THINGS THAT MAKE YOUR CREDIT BAD:

1. MAKING LATE PAYMENTS
As explained earlier, thirty-five percent of your credit score is your payment history. Consistently being late on your credit card payments will drastically hurt your credit score. When you pay your credit card bills on time with the minimum payment due, you safeguard your credit score.

2. NEGLECTING TO PAY AT ALL
Completely ignoring your credit cards bills is much worse than paying late. Each month you miss a credit card payment, you are one month closer to having the account charged off, which will get you an R9 rating, which makes your record look extremely bad.

3. LETTING AN ACCOUNT GET CHARGED OFF

When creditors think that you are not going to pay your credit card bill at all, they charge off the account. This account status looks almost as bad as a foreclosure or bankruptcy!

4. LETTING AN ACCOUNT GET SENT TO COLLECTIONS

Creditors often use third-party debt collectors to try and collect payment from you. Creditors may send your account to collections before or after charging it off. A collection status shows that the creditor gave up trying to get payment from you and hired someone else to do it. Not good.

5. DEFAULTING ON A LOAN

Loan defaults are similar to credit card charge-offs. A default shows that you have not fulfilled your end of the loan agreement. If this is on your Credit Report, you can pretty much forget getting a loan from any lender or creditor.

6. FILING BANKRUPTCY (More on this later)

This is one of two of the worse things you can have on your Credit Report. Bankruptcy will devastate your credit score. It is a good idea to seek alternatives like consumer credit counseling before filing bankruptcy.

7. FORECLOSURE (More on this later)

This is the second of two of worse things you can have on your Credit Report. Getting behind on your mortgage payments will lead your lender to eventually foreclose on your home. In turn, the late payments will hurt your credit score and make it harder to get approved for future mortgage loans.

8. GETTING A JUDGMENT AGAINST YOU

A judgment shows you not only avoided your bills, but that the court had to get involved to make you pay the debt. While they both hurt your credit score, a paid judgment is better than an unpaid one.

9. HIGH CREDIT CARD BALANCES

The second most important part of your credit score is the level of debt, measured by credit utilization. Having high credit card balances (relative to your credit limit) increases your credit utilization and decreases your credit score.

10. MAXED OUT CREDIT CARDS

Maxed out and over-the-limit credit card balances make your credit utilization percentage very high. This is not good for your credit score.

11. CLOSING CREDIT CARDS THAT STILL HAVE BALANCES

When you close a credit card that still has a balance, your credit limit drops to $0 while your balance remains. This makes it look like you have maxed out your credit card, causing your credit score to fall hard.

12. CLOSING OLD CREDIT CARDS

As has been stated, 15% of your credit score is the length of your credit history. Old credit cards work in your favor and look good on your Credit Report. Closing old credit cards, especially your oldest card, makes your credit history seem shorter than it really is.

13. APPLYING FOR SEVERAL CREDIT CARDS OR LOANS

Credit inquiries account for 10% of your credit score decline. Making several credit or loan applications within a short period of time will cause your credit score to drop. Keep applications to a minimum.

14. HAVING ONLY CREDIT CARDS OR ONLY LOANS

A mix of credit is 10% of your credit score. When you have only one type of credit account, either loans or credit cards, your credit score could be affected. This factor mostly comes into play when you don't have much other credit information in your credit history.

15. CO-SIGNING FOR SOMEONE

Never co-sign for anyone if you can help it! By cosigning, you are accepting FULL RESPONSIBILITY for the other person's debt, and if the other person does not pay as agreed, YOU are responsible for paying whatever they didn't pay. A cosigned account will appear on both Credit Reports. This significantly impacts your credit score. Keep in mind that you can do anything that you set your mind to do and if you set your mind to become financially disciplined in order to begin building your financial future, you will be!

FINANCIAL TIPS TO REMEMBER:

➢ Like every other recurring item in your budget, the Emergency Fund is something you put money into each month until you reach your desired goal.

➢ If you currently do not have an Emergency Fund or find it difficult to save, the key is to start small. Even if you only start with $10.00 in the beginning, at least you have taken the initiative to start.

➢ View your emergency fund as an insurance policy and guard it carefully. Do not dip into it for incidental expenses. Use it only for the purpose in which it was intended – for emergencies, and pray that an emergency never happens.

➢ It is not smart to use credit cards for things that you consume quickly or are non-essential, such as meals, groceries or clothes or shoes.

➢ If you keep your standard of living *below* what you earn, you will not have to cut back to save money, instead, you will have excess cash flow because you will earn more than you need to live on.

Your Credit Report

A person's credit report is one of the most important tools consumers can use to maintain their financial security and credit rating, but for so long many did not know how to obtain one, or what to do with the information it provided.

~Ruben Hinojosa

*P*eople have become increasingly dependent on credit, but you must understand that credit is not a cash substitute but rather a loan that you must pay back in a reasonable amount of time with interest. Credit is receiving something without fully paying for it at the time that you get it. It can be defined as faith in your ability and intention to pay for or pay back what has been borrowed or purchased. The level of confidence that a lender has in you will depend on a variety of things. Your income is a main factor indicating whether or not you will be able to pay back the loan. Before a decision is made, the amount of debt you already have is another main factor taken into account. The amount of borrowing that you have already done and how well you made those payments is another indicator of your intention and ability to pay back what you are seeking to borrow. All this information determines what interest rates you will be given and how long you will have to pay back the loan. The terms of your debt repayment include the interest percentage. The interest on credit is usually expressed as an Annual Percentage Rate (APR). The APR usually appears in the "terms" section of the Credit Application and takes into account how long it will take you to pay back the loan. Your Credit Report is the first thing that lenders look at when you apply for a credit card or want to make a major purchase. However, your Credit Report is not only looked at by credit card and loan organizations, but it is also viewed by landlords, insurance companies, the military and even potential employers. Many employers conduct credit checks as a part of the hiring process. If you haven't demonstrated financial responsibility in the past, a potential employer might be hesitant to hire you because they may believe that your level of debt is too high for the salary being offered. These companies review your Credit Report for the sole purpose of making a determination of whether you are responsible or not. Lenders offer better terms and lower interest rates to consumers with good credit scores. Building a good credit record is a crucial step in reaching financial independence and can be established by doing the following:

- Paying all your bills on time
- Making (at least) the minimum payment due
- Keeping low balances on your credit cards

Being responsible with the use of credit also means living within your financial means. You do not need to keep up with the Jones'. You should compare the size of the home you buy or the car you drive by the size of the monthly payment you can comfortably afford and not the size of what someone else has. This is being wise and responsible.

WHAT IS A CREDIT REPORT?
If you have not begun to do so, it is time to start thinking about the importance of your Credit Report. Your Credit Report is a detailed record of your payment history with lenders and is an indicator that reflects how well or badly you

manage your financial matters. Your Credit Report is maintained by companies known as Credit Bureaus. As mentioned earlier, creditors and lenders use your Credit Report to make decisions on whether or not to loan you money. After approving you, the lender/creditor submits information regarding your paying strength to the credit bureaus. This information includes how much you borrowed, how much you have paid back so far, your credit limit, the type of account you have, date the account was opened and whether the account has been delinquent. Accounts that have been sent to collections are also placed on your Credit Report. Public records such as bankruptcies, tax liens, foreclosures, or lawsuit judgments appear on your Credit Report too. The most damaging marks to have on your Credit Report are bankruptcies and foreclosures. Finally, your Credit Report includes inquiries that are placed when you make an application for credit. Inquires will be explained more later on in the chapter.

Personal information like your name, current and previous addresses and current and previous employers also appear on your Credit Report, but not your race, marital status, religious beliefs, political affiliation, savings or checking account information, and/or any arrest records.

CREDIT BUREAUS

A credit bureau is an agency that gathers information on how consumers use their credit and how they pay back what they borrowed. Credit bureaus collect your information from as many financial transactions or inquiries as they can. Then they sell access to that information to anyone who has a legally-recognized and legitimate reason to use your information. In case you didn't know it, one of the major purposes of credit bureaus is to sell your information to companies and organizations looking to send out credit offers. It works like this:

1. A credit card company wants to promote a new type of credit card.

2. The credit card company will contact the credit bureaus and request a profile of the kind of person they think would be interested in their new card. The profile might include things like credit score, income level, amount of debt, number of credit cards, etc.

3. The credit bureaus then search through their records looking for individuals that match that particular profile. If you fit the profile, an application is mailed to you or someone may call you on the phone promoting the offer. It is just one of the ways that credit bureaus make their money.

CREDIT REPORTING AGENCIES

In the United States, there are three top credit bureaus that are used to determine a person's creditworthiness. Those credit bureaus are **Experian, TransUnion, and Equifax**. Understanding how these credit bureaus calculate your FICO score can help you build and keep a high score. There are not very many differences among the three main credit bureaus. All three are used effectively with minor variations in the manner in which they organize your report. All three however are pretty reliable.

Equifax

Their headquarters are located in Atlanta, GA. They also operate in Latin American and Europe. Equifax provides consumer and business credit information as well as fraud protection and marketing services. Equifax manages credit data on over 350 million American consumers.

Experian

Experian's headquarters are located in Costa Mesa, CA. They also operate out of Dublin, Ireland. According to the company's website, Experian manages credit data on about 215 million American consumers. When you request a credit score from Experian, you will receive not only a score, but also an explanation of what the number represents in terms of how lenders will view your creditworthiness.

TransUnion

TransUnion was founded in 1968 in Chicago, IL, which is currently where their headquarters is located. The company was originally a railcar leasing firm, later expanding into data collection and consumer credit. According to the company, TransUnion operates in 25 countries and holds credit information on about 500 million people.

Credit Bureau Contact Information

Here are the main addresses and telephone numbers for each of the three major credit bureaus.

EQUIFAX	EXPERIAN	TRANSUNION
P.O. Box 740241 Atlanta, GA 30374 1-800-685-1111	P.O. Box 2002 Allen, TX 75013 1-888-397-3742	P.O. Box 1000 Chester, PA 19022 1-800-888-4213

WHY YOUR CREDIT SCORE IS IMPORTANT

When you apply for a credit card, mortgage loan, cell phone, or are trying to get a car financed, your credit record is reviewed. Credit reporting makes it possible for stores to accept your checks, for banks to issue credit or debit cards to you and for corporations to manage their operations. Depending on your credit score, lenders will determine what risk you pose to them.

Basically, if you have a poor credit score, lenders will not completely reject you (unless your credit is utterly awful); instead, they will lend you money at a higher annual percentage rate verses someone with a better credit score. The table below shows how individuals with varying credit scores will pay drastically different interest rates on similar mortgage amounts. The difference in interest includes a large impact on the monthly payments, which
includes both interest and principal.

Score	Rate	Monthly Payment
720-850	5.49%	$851
700-719	5.61%	$862
675-699	6.15%	$914
620-674	7.30%	$1,028
560-619	8.53%	$1,157
500-559	9.29%	$1,238

Source: myfico.com

WHAT IS A FICO SCORE?

A FICO (Fair Isaac Corporation) Score is calculated based on the information contained in your Credit Report. The numbers are generated by a computer program that runs through your Report. It looks for patterns, characteristics, and red flags in your credit history. Based on what the program finds, it spits out a score. Scores typically range from 350 to 850 with higher numbers being much better. The more negative information you have on your Credit Report, the lower your score will be. The higher your credit score, the better loan and interest rates you will qualify for. The amount of money you pay in interest could amount to hundreds of thousands of dollars over your lifetime. This is money you could be saving, contributing towards your retirement, or passing on to your children to help build multi-generational wealth.

Credit bureaus have a ton of information about you in their databases, and it is difficult for lenders to sort through it all. The credit bureaus individually calculate your FICO score based on the credit history they have on file for you. This means you can have up to three different FICO scores at one time (from three different credit bureaus), but they are usually similar in score ranges. Your credit score changes as the information on your Credit Report changes. Therefore, it can change often since new information is added to your Credit Report all the time.

WHAT MAKES UP A CREDIT SCORE?

A fico score takes into account a lot of different information from your Credit Report, but it is not all weighted equally. Some aspects of your credit history are more important than others and will weigh more heavily on your overall score. Your FICO score is essentially made up of the following:

- Payment History – 35%
- Total Amounts Owed – 30%
- Length of Credit History – 15%
- New Credit – 10%
- Type of Credit in Use – 10%

PAYMENT HISTORY (35%)

The bulk of your credit score comes from your payment history and how much debt you actually have. Payment history traditionally has been the largest factor in determining your credit score. Prior to 2009, 35% of your credit score was based on your payment history. Paying on time can still make the difference between average and exceptional credit, but now one late payment won't hurt you as much as it did in the past. If you have a history of paying your accounts on time, but have an occasional late payment, this will not be as detrimental as it used to.

Since this category has such a big impact on your overall credit score, if you go through a foreclosure (or short sale) it will not just be the foreclosure that adversely impacts your credit, but also the months of late payments that precede the foreclosure. Those two items, payment history and total amounts owed account for 65% of your credit score! So, if you are really looking to improve your credit score, these are the two main areas that you want to make sure is in tact.

AMOUNT OWED COMPARED TO AVAILABLE CREDIT (30%)

As mentioned above, the next major component, which accounts for 30% of your credit score, is the amount of revolving debt you owe in relation to your available balances. It is calculated on an individual account basis as well as an overall basis. As it stands today, your overall debt will play a bigger role in your credit score than it has in the past. It may now even have a bigger affect on your credit score than your payment history. To avoid this, try not to use more than 50% of your available balance from any lender. Ideally you want to borrow less than 33% of your available balances. This means contrary to popular belief, it is better to owe a smaller amount on several cards than to max one card to its limit.

LENGTH OF CREDIT HISTORY (15%)

Try and keep a credit card open at least seven years. Your length of credit history comprises about 15% of your score. People with credit scores over 800 typically hold at least three credit cards with low balances, which they have had open for over seven years each. Rather than closing accounts, it is best to work toward paying them off, and then let the accounts remain open with a small amount of activity that is paid off each month.

INQUIRIES AND NEW DEBT (10%)

Inquiries and new debt does lower your score. Inquirers do not look good because it indicates to lenders that you may be soon taking on new debt. The good news is if you are shopping for a house, all mortgage inquiries within thirty days of each other will be grouped as one inquiry; for autos, it is a fourteen day limit. In 2009, inquiries for new debt will have less of an effect than they used to.

TYPE OF DEBT (10%)

The last 10% of your score is based on the type of credit: installment vs. revolving debt. Installment debt, such as an auto loan, is looked upon more favorably than revolving debt. A credit card is considered revolving debt. In addition, with the 2009 changes, you now get points for your ability to successfully manage multiple types of debt; i.e. a mortgage, auto loan and credit cards.

Here is how the weighting breaks down in the form of a pie graph:

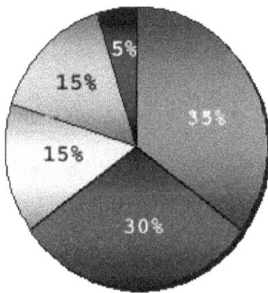

35% - Previous Credit Performance
30% - Current Level of Indebtedness
15% - Time Credit has been in use
15% - Types of Credit Available
5% - Pursuit of New Credit

As you can see by the pie graph, your credit rating is most affected by your historical inclination for paying off your debts. The factor that can boost your credit rating the most is having a past that shows you pay off your debts fairly quickly. Additionally, maintaining low levels of debt, having a long credit history, and refraining from constantly applying for additional credit will all help your credit score.

R1 and R9 are notes left on your Credit Reports by your creditors. These notes are used to indicate the status of the credit items on your report. An R1 means that the account is a revolving account in good standing. An R9 means a revolving account in very poor standing. R1s and R9s are two extremes of the many account classifications that your creditors can add to your Credit Report. Each of these classifications consist of two parts, the account type and the account status. On your Credit Report, "R" refers to a "revolving" credit account, "I" refers to an individual account and "M" refers to a mortgage account. These classifications then include a rating supplied by the creditor who reported the item. It is their rating of you as a borrower. There are only two ratings which are not negative. A rating of "1" is good and a rating of "0" means there is no history or not enough history on you to be able to rate you. Every other rating, "2" through "9" is considered negative. Creditors look at these ratings, the late payment and other notations such as charge offs or collections.

The Fair Credit Reporting Act (FCRA) requires that most negative credit items remain on your credit record for no more than seven years, except for bankruptcy, which stays on your report up to ten years and in rare cases even longer. Inquiries may remain on a Credit Report for up to two years. It is important to note that these two years, seven years and ten year terms are the time limits for reporting negative credit. Your creditors or the credit bureaus can choose to have the negative credit information deleted whenever there is a reason to do so.

You must know what you are looking at when you have that credit record in your hand. There are different codes and they each mean something different.

SECTIONS OF YOUR CREDIT REPORT
Your Credit Report is divided into six main sections:

- consumer demographic information (address, birthday and employment)
- consumer statement
- account histories
- public records
- inquiries
- creditor contacts.

On the next page is a table that shows what the "R" codes mean on your Credit Report.

R1-R9 Credit Codes

R	REVOLVING
0	Little or no credit history
1	Paid as agreed
2	30+ days past due
3	60+ days past due
4	90+ days past due
5	120+ days past the due date
6	This rating does not exist
7	Making regular payments under wage earner plan (popular name for a debt repayment plan under Chapter 13 of the Bankruptcy Code.)
8	Repossession
9	Charge off to bad debt

Your goal is to earn all "R1s" on your Credit Report!

When you open a new account, miss a payment, or move, these sections are updated with new information. Stated already, derogatory records will stay on your Credit Report for 7-10 years! That's a long time. Favorable records can remain on your Credit Report longer. Not all creditors report to all three agencies. The agencies obtain their data independently so your reports from Equifax, Experian, and TransUnion could be slightly different from each other. That is why it is important to check your three Credit Reports every 6-12 months to ensure that the information is accurate and up-to-date. Paying bills on time is generally the single most important contributor to a good credit score. Being late on any bill, for any length of time, is a possible indication of future nonpayment of debt and is almost always viewed negatively by lenders.

If your application for credit is denied, you are entitled to a free Credit Report. The denial letter you receive should list the credit bureau used to obtain your information. Contact that agency for the copy the report. If you do not understand the report, contact the credit bureau or your local consumer credit counselor. Under recent federal law, they must give you one free annual Credit Report.

REQUESTING A COPY OF YOUR CREDIT REPORT

The best method of obtaining your Credit Report is to send a written request. Make sure that you ask for your credit score as well (not just the report) because the Credit Report and the credit score are two different things. You can also request a copy online at www.annualcreditreport.com. Each agency requires you to enter specific information verifying who you are (including your social security number) before they will release any information to you. They may also request a payment of $8.00 or more depending on the state. You are exempt from paying the fee if you are getting your free annual Credit Report, or were denied credit in the last sixty days, receive public assistance, are unemployed and plan to seek employment in the next 60 days, or you believe you are a victim of fraud. When writing a letter requesting your report, provide your full name (first, middle, and last) social security number, date of birth, current address and how long you have been living there, any previous addresses (if current address is less than two years), current employer, and home and work phone numbers. After proving the requested information, you should receive your credit report is the specified time frame given.

FINANCIAL TIPS TO REMEMBER:

➢ Your Credit Report is the first thing that lenders look at when you apply for a credit card or want to make a major purchase.

➢ Lenders offer better terms and lower interest rates to consumers with good credit scores.

➢ Your Credit Report is a detailed record of your payment history with lenders and is an indicator that reflects how well or badly you manage your financial matters.

➢ A credit bureau is an agency that gathers information on how consumers use their credit and how they pay back what they borrowed.

➢ A FICO (Fair Isaac Corporation) Score is calculated based on the information contained in your Credit Report. The numbers are generated by a computer program that runs through your Report. It looks for patterns, characteristics, and red flags in your credit history.

Become Financially Literate

Money is like a sixth sense and you can't make use of the other five without it."

~William Somerset Maugham

aking money is one thing, but saving a percentage of the money you make and making it grow is another. As I have already said, it is not about how much money you make, but much of your money you save or invest that makes the difference. If you make a six figured salary, but you have nothing to show for it, then what is the point in making six figures? With a six figured salary, you should own a home (mortgage), have a car, a retirement account, an Emergency Fund and a nice size savings account. You should also be able to show that you have made some valuable long-term investments. Financial management and investing are lifelong endeavors. Making sound financial decisions is important for achieving the financial goals that you have set for yourself. The more knowledgeable and experienced you are in financial matters, the fewer mistakes you will make and the less costly it will be for you. Read books on personal finances and retirement planning so that you will know how to make the most of your money. Books that I have read and found to be financially enlightening as well as practical to implement are: Smart Women Finish Rich (David Bach); Rich Dad Poor Dad (Robert Kiyosaki); Richest man in Babylon (George S. Clason); The Automatic Millionaire (David Bach); and The Millionaire Next Door (Thomas Stanley and William Danko). Stay on top of your finances. Know what is going on with your money and find the best ways to invest it. Smart people finish rich!

STOP THE EMOTIONAL SPENDING!

I have heard some people say that shopping makes them feel better when they are feeling down. This is called "emotional spending" and it occurs when people buy things they really do not need or want because they think it will make them feel better. Some people resort to this when they are feeling depressed, have anxiety, are frustrated, stressed, bored, feel under-appreciated, are feeling inferior, etc. This is not a good habit because the money is literally being "used" as a scapegoat and is virtually being "wasted" on non-essentials. If you are one of those people, it is imperative that you find another way to deal with your emotions other than spending money frivolously. Inanimate objects can never make you feel better anyway, because the essence of who you are is spirit and material things can not satisfy the spirit part of who you are.

It is also wise to be psychologically stable when you go shopping. For instance, never go to the grocery store when you are hungry. If you do, you will purchase too much food. Never shop for something to wear the day before the event. You will either spend too much money on it, or compromise on something you really do not like. Never buy a car when you are desperate for transportation. You will end up paying too much money for it and/or buy something you really are not crazy about. The bottom line is that you should always be level-headed when you shop. Be in a state of mind where you can take it or leave it and be alright with your decision. You must be held accountable for your spending.

If there are certain things that you want, then you should plan for them. For instance, if you want a new computer, but it is not an emergency, then budget a computer into your Spending Plan and set a target date to buy it. When you develop your New Year Goals (not New Year's Resolutions), you can have an area for things that you desire to purchase within the new year. That way, you have it in your mind that you will be budgeting that/those things into your Spending Plan throughout the year. Impulse Spending is not very smart, nor will it get you to your goal of becoming financial independent.

PAY ATTENTION TO WHERE YOUR MONEY GOES

Often the things that we view in life as small purchases can make the difference between being a millionaire and being broke. Once you calculate how much that morning bagel and cup of coffee really costs, you will realize that making small, manageable changes in your everyday expenses can have just as big of an impact on your financial situation as getting a raise. Let's take a look at how much that morning bagel and cup of coffee really costs:

Bagel	$1.63
Coffee	$1.49
	$3.12
Weekly	$21.84
Monthly	$87.36
Yearly	$1,048.32
Five Years	$5,241.60

When you do not actually *see* how the money is adding up, it is easier to spend it, but when you can look at it this way, it becomes clear and shocking. That same $3.12 can be put towards your Emergency Fund, which will give you a minimum of $1,048.32 at the end of the year and the amounts above do not even include tax. Go figure! As far as your morning bagel and coffee goes, you can buy yourself a whole bag of bagels for $3.89 and a can of coffee or $2.99 and eat and drink at home every morning. Another good way to keep up with your spending is to keep receipts for everything you spend. This will make it more real to you in terms of what you really spend. Try it. For one month save every receipt of everything you purchase, from a pack of gum, to a new shirt, to ink for your printer. Write each expense down and at the end of the month, tally up what you have spent and take a good look at just where most of your money goes. food? clothes? electronics? your hair? This technique will definitely expose your spending habits.

A FINANCING OVERVIEW

Financing basically means to borrow money from a bank so that you can make a big purchase. Financing is a means of obtaining money, then paying the loan back in a specified time period for a set monthly amount. Upon approval, the bank will pay the merchant the total cost for what you are buying and they (the bank) will send you a bill each month. The bank will only lend you the money if you agree to pay interest on top of the money they loaned you. When you agree, you have established some form of credit. In most cases, people turn to financing when buying a house, a car, or a boat; but there are instances when financing is needed to purchase furniture or computers as well as other electronic accessories. People are even financing cosmetic surgery these days.

Most Americans could not afford homes or cars without the ability to borrow. The average Jane and Joe Blow do not have $215,000 in their savings account to purchase their first home. Financing makes obtaining these things more affordable than they otherwise would be. Borrowing is frequently justified for automobiles, homes, work or recreational vehicles, education, home improvements and other purchases that will have a value lasting beyond the time it takes to pay them off.

CREDIT CARDS

Credit cards can be your best friend or your worst enemy. For many, these small rectangles of plastic have become a financial nightmare because they have gotten many people entangled in mountain high debt. But as with everything, when you learn how to make these small pieces of plastic work for you, you will become an exception to the rule.

Receiving your first credit card in the mail is a very exciting time and it puts a big smile on your face. You feel a sense of adulthood and are ready to go out and shop 'til you drop. It is a natural feeling; but before you go shopping, you need to STOP. THINK, and RATIONALIZE. Instead of going on a shopping spree, why not put the credit card in a safe place and act as though you never received it? You will have the security that if an emergency does come up, you have a backup with an available balance. A credit card is a great financial backup and having the credit available for emergencies is definitely a life-saver, but your credit card should only be used for emergencies. The temptation to use a credit card over cash is very strong, but I will advise that if you have the cash to pay for something, use the cash.

Many college-aged students (and also adults) do not fully understand the facts and fees involved in their credit cards and haphazardly use them for almost everything, as though they were debit cards. There is a big difference between a credit card and a debit card. For one, a debit card is equivalent to using cash because the money comes directly out of your checking account. The card should not go through if the money is not in your account, although it does sometimes happen. However, you do not pay interest on the items you buy when you use your debit card, but when you use your credit card, there is interest added on to the principal balance.

Unfortunately, when you buy things with credit cards, you don't feel the immediate significance of your spending because you see no cash changing hands.

There are certain facts that you need to know about credit cards and the more knowledgeable you are of these facts, the better off you will be in terms of using your card(s) to your advantage. Below are the advantages, disadvantages, responsibilities and facts about that you should know about credit cards. This information is extremely relevant to learn for your own credit card health.

Credit Card Advantages:
- ✓ Able to get essential items right away if you do not have the available cash
- ✓ No need to carry cash
- ✓ Creates a record of purchases
- ✓ Easier than writing checks
- ✓ Improves your credit every time you make an on-time minimum payment

Credit Card Disadvantages:
- ✓ You pay interest on everything you buy
- ✓ May pay additional fees, including annual fees
- ✓ The available credit may increase the impulse to buy things you do not really need
- ✓ When you open a new credit card account, you make an impact on your credit score, reducing 5 points from the fico score with each new card

Your Credit Card Responsibilities:
- ✓ Spend only what you can repay
- ✓ Read and understand your credit card contract
- ✓ Pay at least the minimum amount due on time
- ✓ Know your interest rates
- ✓ Notify your creditor if you cannot meet payments
- ✓ Report lost or stolen credit cards immediately

- ✓ Never give your card number over the phone unless you initiated the call or are certain of the caller's identity
- ✓ Get a credit card with the lowest interest rate possible and no annual fees
- ✓ Read the fine print located on the back of your billing statement and yearly disclosure statement.

Credit Card Facts:

- ✓ The industry is dominated by six major companies: Bank of America, J.P. Morgan, Chase, Citigroup, Capital One, Discover, and American Express. They account for about 90% of all credit card debt.
- ✓ As of 2007, 78% of all American households had credit cards and 60% of these households carried a balance.
- ✓ Statistics show that 78% of college students had at least one credit card. Nearly 40% of Freshman students sign-up for credit cards and almost 20% get them in high school.
- ✓ Of the 78% who have credit cards, 32% have 4 or more cards
- ✓ It would take roughly 12 years for a student to pay off a $1,000 credit card debt with an 18% interest rate if they are only making minimum payments.
- ✓ Banks that specialize in credit cards have been much more profitable than banks in general. According to FDIC data for 2007, the return on equity was 15.1% for credit card banks, compared to 8.2% for all banks.
- ✓ Credit card companies collected $115 billion in revenue in 2006, about two-thirds from interest payments, one-fifth from fees paid by merchants who accept the cards, and about 15% from consumer fees.

✓ When you are attempting to pay off credit card debt, always pay the credit card with the highest rate of interest first

Credit Card Accountability, Responsibility and Disclosure Act of 2009:

With the failing economy, Americans are being strongly encouraged to eliminate debt in what is now being considered the new normal. The President Obama Administration passed *the Credit Card Accountability, Responsibility and Disclosure Act of 2009* for the purpose of attempting to remove those unfriendly terms that kept Americans in debt. A major centerpiece of the bill was designed to protect college-aged students from piling up debt as they enter the workforce.

Below are the main components of the bill. This should be good news to students, parents and consumers.

1. MUST HAVE A NOTE FROM YOUR PARENTS
Parents will have to co-sign the Credit Card Application for any student under the age of 21. The only exception to this is for those under 21 who can prove that they are able to repay their balance by providing employment or financial verification. Any credit limit increase will also require a co-signer's written approval.

2. NO MORE FREE GIVEAWAYS FOR FILLING OUT AN APPLICATION
Under the new law, a credit card company cannot offer free gifts for filling out an application unless its representatives are at least 1,000 feet away from a college campus. In the past, it was the norm for Credit Card Companies to have tables set up with all sort of free items: umbrellas, T-Shirts, water bottles, etc. All a student needed to do was fill out an application in order to get one of those free items. No more.

3. NO MORE SECRET DEALS

Many are surprised to hear that colleges and universities have often entered into marketing or promotional agreements with credit card companies. In the past these agreements were not disclosed to the public, but now disclosure is a requirement. These agreements often involved the college or university getting a percentage of the revenue generated by the credit card companies. In exchange, the educational institution allowed its logo to be placed on the card. Under the new law, colleges and universities, as well as alumni associations, must file disclosure statements detailing their promotional agreements.

4. NO RELEASE OF CREDIT REPORTS FOR STUDENTS UNDER AGE 21

The CARD Act of 2009 now prohibits Credit Reporting agencies from providing reports to credit card companies on individuals under 21 years of age, unless they are given permission to do so from the individual. This will severely limit the amount of pre-approved credit card offers that college students receive.

5. NO MORE OVER-THE-LIMIT FEES

Unless the consumer "opts-in", a credit card company is no longer allowed to charge over-the-limit credit card fees. If the consumer does not opt-in, any charge that would result in a balance above the credit limit would be rejected at the time of purchase. Additionally, the over-the-limit fee cannot exceed the balance that is over the card limit. If a customer is $15.00 over the limit, the fee cannot exceed $15.00.

6. LATE FEES CAPPED

For those who occasionally pay their credit card bill late, the late fee cannot exceed $25. Be warned, though, that there is no fee restriction for those who are late more than once in a six-month period.

As I close this chapter I would like to reiterate the importance of maintaining good credit. Remember that it takes seven years for basic derogatory information to be removed from your Credit Report, ten years for bankruptcies and two years for inquiries so be careful. Guard your credit as though it were your livelihood, because ultimately, it is the foundation of your financial health.

WHAT IS A BANKRUPTCY?

Bankruptcy is an option that is considered when the debt of a person, company or organization becomes too much to pay. Bankruptcy laws help people who can no longer pay their creditors get a fresh start by liquidating assets to pay their debts or by creating a repayment plan. Bankruptcy laws also protect troubled businesses and provide for orderly distributions to creditors through reorganization or liquidation. Bankruptcy is a very serious matter. Declaring your self bankrupt can have disastrous long-term implications. The actual Bankruptcy Code of the United States is called Title 11 and has various chapters within it. For example, Chapter 7 deals with the process of liquidation bankruptcy. Chapter 11 controls the reorganization of a business that is no longer able to pay their debts and Chapter 13 has to do with restructuring your debt.

Most cases are filed under the three main chapters of the Bankruptcy Code : Chapter 7, Chapter 11, and Chapter 13. Federal courts have exclusive jurisdiction over bankruptcy cases. This means that a bankruptcy case cannot be filed in a state court. A first time bankrupt will generally receive discharge one year after the date of the bankruptcy order. In some cases, the bankruptcy discharge period will be less than one year. A bankruptcy is a public record and has a bad stigma attached to the name.

**Differences Between
Chapter 7, 11, and 13 Bankruptcies**

Chapter 7

Generally speaking, a Chapter 7 bankruptcy means the selling off of your valuable assets in order to pay your debts. It does not mean that all of your debt is eliminated entirely. It means that all "unsecured" debt does not have to be paid back, but the "secured" debt must be dealt with in some kind of way. In a chapter 7 bankruptcy, the debtor turns over all non-exempt property to the bankruptcy trustee who converts it to cash for distribution to the creditors. The debtor receives a discharge of all dischargeable debts usually within four months. While there are limitations to what can be confiscated by creditors, (such as your home under the homestead protection), expect that creditors will sell off most of your valued possessions to pay part of your debts off. The effect of the filing is to discharge someone burdened with debt from having to pay it all back. It also stops creditors or other collection agencies from harassing you with telephone calls, letters, and/or personal contact in an effort to get you to pay the debt you owe them.

To be eligible to file a Chapter 7 bankruptcy, the person filing has to live or have a residence in the United States. In addition, they can not have been a debtor in a bankruptcy case in the 180 day period prior to filing the current bankruptcy case. They must receive counseling from an approved nonprofit credit counseling agency prior to the filing and pass the "Median Family Income" Test. They may not have received a Chapter 7 bankruptcy discharge in the previous eight years or a Chapter 13 discharge in the previous six years.

Chapter 13

Unlike Chapter 7, a Chapter 13 filing means that you acknowledge what you owe to your creditors and are restructuring your debt by negotiating with your creditors to establish a payment plan to pay what is owed in three to five years. Chapter 13 is a formal declaration that you are willingly working with creditors so that they will get their money, but at a slightly slower rate than they might have wanted. By promising to pay off your debts, you are allowed to keep valuable personal items rather than turning them over to be sold. In a similar way, taking this step can limit some of the damage to your credit score that is incurred with filing for bankruptcy. Typically the arrangement reached with creditors in a Chapter 13, is to have you pay the regular monthly payments, plus an additional amount that will get you caught up on your payments over time.

There are costs and also some benefits to whichever bankruptcy approach you decide to take. On the one hand, filing Chapter 7 offers the freedom to eradicate the heavy debt that is currently hanging over you, while Chapter 13 offers you the chance to restructure that debt in order to be more manageable for you. Chapter 7 means the liquidation of almost all your valuables as well as the total devastation to your credit rating, whereas Chapter 13 allows you to keep many of your possessions while keeping your credit score in tact.

To be eligible to file a Chapter 13 bankruptcy the person must reside in the United States, have a regular income, have unsecured debt less than $336,900 and secured debt less than $1,010,650. They must also receive counseling from an approved non-profit credit counseling agency. In order to obtain a discharge in a Chapter 13 bankruptcy, an individual must not have been granted a discharge in a Chapter 7 bankruptcy in the previous 4 years or been granted a Chapter 13 discharge in the last 2 years.

Chapter 11

When a business finds that it is no longer able to pay its creditors or maintain its debts, it can file for protection under Chapter 11 in a Bankruptcy Court. A Chapter 11 filing means that the business intends to continue operating while the bankruptcy court supervises the company's debt and contractual obligations. The court has the power to cancel all or some of the company's debts. The company can then make a fresh start without having the financial burden hanging over their head. Chapter 11 Bankruptcy is the usual choice for large businesses seeking to restructure their debt. This chapter of the Bankruptcy code controls the reorganization of a business that is no longer able to pay their debts. However, it is available to individuals, corporations and partnerships for filing. It has no limits on the amount of debt, as Chapter 13 does. Chapter 11 is probably the most flexible of all the chapters, but its flexibility makes it generally more expensive to the debtor. The rate of successful Chapter 11 reorganizations is low, sometimes estimated at 10% or less.

Your credit rating will be devastated by any kind of bankruptcy, but a chapter 13 looks a little better on your credit record than a 7. When you file for a bankruptcy, you are saying to the world that you are no longer worthy to be trusted with future credit and with a bankruptcy on your Credit Report, it becomes almost impossible to get a new mortgage, a car loan, a credit card, and/or it even limits very small forms of credit such as appliance financing. Because of the many drawbacks of filing for bankruptcy, many individuals in need of debt relief look for other options.

To avoid having to even consider bankruptcy, be very responsible with how you spend money. Living within or below your means will safeguard you from getting overwhelmed with debt. If you apply good money matters now, you will have enough money saved or invested to purchase things with cash, which is so much easier than having bills upon bills to pay and then getting entangled with the cycle of late payments, bill collectors and bad credit.

FINANCIAL TIPS TO REMEMBER:

✓ It is not about how much money you make, but much of your money you save or invest.

- ✓ Financing is a means of obtaining money, then paying the loan back in a specified time period for a set monthly amount.

- ✓ A credit card is a great financial backup and having the credit available for emergencies is definitely a life-saver, but your credit card should only be used for emergencies.

- ✓ The President Obama Administration passed *the Credit Card Accountability, Responsibility and Disclosure Act of 2009* for the purpose of attempting to remove those unfriendly terms that kept Americans in debt.

- ✓ Declaring your self bankrupt can have disastrous long-term implications.

Plan for Your Future

If you fail to plan, you plan to fail.

~unknown

*R*esearch has shown that those who strategically plan for the future end up with more wealth than those who do not. Wealthy people are planners. They are goal oriented. They have different patterns of thinking than the poor or average person. They set goals and develop plans to achieve those goals without deviating from the plan. For example, if you set a goal to pay off your $3,000 credit card balance and you have developed a plan and set a target date for the final payoff, you will have a better chance of achieving this goal than you would if you merely wished to do it but failed to set a reasonable plan and time table for doing it. Be a planner. Set goals and develop action plans to reach the goals you set. To reach the financial goals that you are setting for yourself, you must set a series of small short-term goals. Every major task is comprised of a group of smaller tasks. When setting those goals, make sure they are measurable and have an identified a target date of completion. You can not win a race if there is no finish line. As you achieve your short-term goals, set more short-term goals. The process of writing down your goals will help you to achieve them. Commit yourself to recording your financial goals on paper. No excuses. Being goal oriented and following an action plan means taking control of your life. It is a vital step towards improving your financial independence.

GO AUTOMATIC

When you get your paycheck, Uncle Sam (the IRS) has already taken his portion out of your check. The biggest income tax you pay is federal withholding. This amount depends upon two main factors: 1.) what tax bracket you fall into and 2.) how many exemptions you claimed on your W4 Form when you were hired. After federal withholding is taken out, there is a 6.2% FICA tax for social security and a 1.45% Medicare tax that is also taken out of your check totaling 7.65 percent (as of this writing). You can not get around paying those. What you have left is your "net" income, which should then be looked at carefully in terms of how much of what is left is spent. The first 10% should always go to you. This is called PAYING YOURSELF FIRST:

> **Pay Yourself 10% First.** (Emergency Fund or Dream Fund). How much you decide to split into each of these individual accounts depends on what you feel has priority over the other. You can also distribute the 10% evenly -50% into each account.

Your rent/mortgage, insurance, utilities, food, credit cards and other bills are all paid *after* you have paid yourself first. There are certain accounts into which you should regularly put your money into as mentioned before: the Emergency Fund, the Retirement Fund and the Dream Fund. The Emergency Fund protects you and your family against the unexpected (job loss, medical emergency, death of a loved one, emergency home repairs, etc). Your retirement fund safeguards your future so you can have more of an income when you are older and will not have to worry so much about making ends meet at a time when you should be relaxing and enjoying the fruit of your labor. Your dream basket enables you to fulfill your desires of traveling, maybe opening a business or pursuing the goals you always wanted. Fund these accounts through automatic withdrawal. When you do it this way, the temptation of spending the money on other things is taken away. You will not have to be disciplined about putting money in and you will have the security of knowing that as long as you don't touch the money in these accounts, they are growing and giving you peace of mind.

Being financially secure enough to enjoy your life in retirement is the last thing on the minds of those under 30, but it is never too early to begin planning for your retirement. However, you absolutely must prepare well in advance and the earlier you start, the better off you will be in the long run. Once you secure the job and the salary that you desire, you must immediately begin to take advantage of the retirement options. Because of the way compound interest works, the sooner you start saving, the less principal you will have to invest in order to end up with the amount you need to retire, and the sooner you will be able to call work an option rather than a necessity. Company-sponsored retirement plans are a particularly great option because you put in pretax dollars and the contribution that the employer gives you tends to be high. Also, companies will often match your contribution, which is like getting free money.

TAKE ADVANTAGE OF YOUR
ORGANIZATION'S RETIREMENT PLAN
Retirement planning is the important task of deciding how you will live after you have stopped working. As a young person, I know that retirement is the very last thing on your mind, but trust me, if you start planning now, you will be

extremely glad you did when you are older, especially when you see how fast and how much your money grows. Before you know it, you will have 20, 25, then 30 years of working under your belt and if you begin investing early, you will have a nice nest egg saved up. The time goes by very fast and that is why it is important to seize every moment and take advantage of smart financial opportunities when they are presented to you. Don't put things off. When you put things off, you are operating in a spirit of procrastination and you do not want to get into that awful habit. As soon as you secure the career you want, you must immediately inquire about the retirement options offered by the company and set up your automatic retirement withdrawals right away! When you make it automatic, you never miss the money. Trust me. You do not miss what you can not see. Investing in your retirement account early is mandatory.

Retirement planning involves the consideration of a number of factors, including what age you hope to retire, how much money you will need to cover your living expenses, things you plan to do once you have retired and where your money will come from. Some people do not want to wait until the legal retirement age of 62 to retire. Some want to retire early – perhaps at 45, 50, or 55 years of age. If this is your case, then you must calculate how much it will take for you to contribute to your retirement account right now, so that when you reach the age that you want to retire, you will be financially secure to do so. However, you must take into account that taking your money out before the age of 59½ will cost you a penalty of 10% or more of the money you have in your retirement account, so take all these things into consideration when working these early retirement plans out.

401K RETIREMENT PLANS

A 401k is a pre-tax retirement plan that is sponsored by an employer usually in public schools and private for-profit companies. The plan enables you to contribute a portion of your earnings before the government takes their usual chunk out of it and place a fixed percentage of your paycheck directly into the 401k account. This qualified retirement plan is one of the most valuable retirement opportunities for working individuals. A primary distinction and excellent benefit of the 401k Plan is the fact that the money invested is tax deferred, meaning that the salary deferrals are pre-taxed until you reach the age of being able to withdraw it. This not only lowers your taxable income, but it also saves you money for retirement tax-free during the working years.

If you happen to leave your current company that offered the 401k plan and you are hired at another organization that offers the same plan, you can do what is called a 401k rollover to your new company. If the new company does not offer the plan, you can roll your money over into a financial institution after you leave a company. If you do this, the account name changes from a 401k Retirement Account into an Individual Retirement Account (IRA) account. As of this writing, there is a limit of $16,500 that you may contribute into your 401k account. This is a before-tax amount. For example, let's say you earn $60,000 a year and you decide to max out your 401k for that year. You will contribute $16,500 from your annual salary of $60,000 and put it into your 401k retirement account. When you file your taxes, your taxable income will only be $43,500 as opposed to the $60,000.

403B RETIREMENT PLANS

Unlike the 401k Plan, 403b participants cannot invest in individual stocks. Instead, their choices are: annuity and variable annuity contracts with insurance companies, a custodial account made up of mutual funds or retirement income accounts for churches. Not-for-profit (tax-exempt) 501c3 employers, such as churches, universities, civil government, tax-exempt hospitals, schools or charities usually offers the 403b Plans, whereas public schools and private for-profit companies offers the 401k Plans.

The key difference between the 401k and 403b plans lie in the investment options. The 401k plan includes any publicly-traded securities (stocks), mutual funds, options, etc. The plan may limit the investments to a selected list prepared by the plan administrator. The 403b investments are limited to annuity contracts or mutual funds and money market funds.

The features of a 401k are very similar to that of a 403b. Employees still contribute part of their salary on a pre-tax basis to the 403b and the employer may match part, all or none of that amount just as in a 401k and both plans have the ability to offer loans to employees. Additionally, the money invested in either your 401k or your 403b grows tax-deferred until you make a withdrawal, which should ideally be at retirement. It is important to note that the "retirement" age in which you can take a penalty-free withdrawal is 59½. If you take money out of your retirement account before this age, you may be subject to a 10% early withdrawal penalty.

ROTH IRAS

A Roth IRA can invest in securities, usually common stocks or mutual funds (although other investments, including derivatives, notes, certificates of deposit, and real estate are possible). As with all IRAs, there are specific eligibility and filing status requirements mandated by the Internal Revenue Service. As of this writing (2010), an individual who is under 50 years of age may contribute a maximum of $5,000 to their Roth IRA, but the limits change from year to year. A person over 50 years of age may contribute up to $6,000 a year under a plan called the Catch up Provision. It is important to note however, that IRS does not allow contributions that are greater than your earnings. This means that the annual amount you earn is the maximum amount you can contribute to a Roth account. Anyone at any age can open a Roth IRA account. Minors may even establish and contribute to a Roth IRA provided the minor has verifiable income.

Some of the eligibility requirements of having a Roth IRA are as follows:

- ✓ If you are a single tax filer your modified adjusted gross income needs to be less than $105,000. Married tax filers need their income to be less than $167,000.

- ✓ The maximum annual contribution is $5,000 per person. Married couples can contribute $10,000. If you are 50 or older

- ✓ You can contribute $6,000 per person annually due to a catch-up provision.

It works something like this. Let's say you invested $5,000 annually over a 20 year period into a Roth IRA and at the end of 20 years, your money grew to $500,000. You may have lost out on the tax deduction on the $100,000, but you do not have to pay any taxes on the $500,000 when you withdraw funds after age 59½ . This can add up to a substantial savings as your earnings increase.

Roth IRA	Traditional IRA
Individuals of all ages can open up a Roth	Must be at least 18 to open up a retirement account
Pay no taxes when you withdraw money at age 59 ½	Pay taxes on the money you withdraw
Contributions can be withdrawn at any time, tax free.	Contributions can be withdrawn at any time, tax free.
Pay a 10% penalty for early withdrawal	Pay a 10% penalty for early withdrawal
There are no required minimum distributions	You have to withdraw a minimum amount
Contributions are NOT tax deductible	Contributions ARE tax deductible
Assets can be passed onto beneficiaries after death.	Assets can be passed onto beneficiaries after death.

THE POWER OF COMPOUNDING

There is a definite reason and a valuable secret why you are being told to start planning for retirement early. The younger you are when you start, the wealthier you will become. How you may ask? Because of the POWER OF COMPOUNDING! What is compounding? Well, I'm glad you asked. Compounding is when the money you make from an initial investment is reinvested to make even more money than the initial investment. Your reinvestment goes back to work to earn you even more money and then even more money. Many people do not realize the power of compounding and the effect of time, but there are some who do understand, and those are the ones who are taking advantage of it and growing richer by the day! The two main factors that will determine how fast your money grows is 1.) the initial investment amount and 2.) the percentage rate.

Let's take a look at how the power of compounding works for the younger person:

Aaron, Bob and Carl all make the intelligent decision to begin planning for retirement. Aaron begins to save at age 20 and puts in $2,000 a year for 10 years. He stops contributing at 30 years old. Carl contributes $2,000 a year until he reaches 65 years of age but he doesn't start saving until he is 40 years old. Bob begins saving at age 30 and also contributes $2,000 a year. He stops when he reaches age 65. Neither of the last two will have as much money at retirement as Aaron, even though he only contributed for 10 years. Both Bob and Carl contributed for 25 years but still do not have as much money as Aaron, thanks to the power of compounding. Assuming a growth rate of 8 percent each year, as the chart below shows, both Bob and Carl contributed considerably more money than Aaron, but will end up with $100,000 to $300,000 less than Aaron 65 years of age, whereas Aaron can stop contributing at age 30. It pays to begin saving early!

Example of Compounding of Savings at 8 Percent

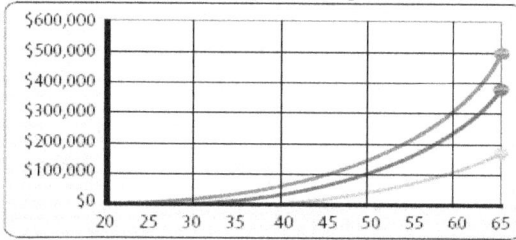

$600,000	○ Aaron begins saving at age 20, saves $2,000 for 10 years. (sets aside $20,000)
$500,000	
$400,000	○ Bob begins saving at age 30, saves $2,000 for 35 years. (sets aside $70,000)
$300,000	
$200,000	
$100,000	○ Carl begins saving at age 40, saves $2,000 for 25 years. (sets aside $50,000)
$0	

20 25 30 35 40 45 50 55 60 65

The secret that makes the rich get richer is this: If you put your money in an investment that delivers a good return and then reinvest those earnings as you receive them, the snowball effect can be astounding over the long term. This is particularly true in retirement accounts where principal is allowed to grow for years tax-deferred or even tax-free, such as a 401k, 403b, or Roth IRA.

AN INTERESTING TALE THAT ILLUSTRATES THE POWER OF COMPOUNDING

No one could beat Rafael playing Chess. He was the greatest chess player in the entire country. The King brought people in from near and far who were considered chess gurus to try and see if they could beat Rafael, but none of them could. The king was so delighted to have a chess genius in his kingdom that he offered Rafael anything he wanted, including one of his own daughters to wed. He gave Rafael 24 hours to think about what his request would be. After that, he was to return and make his request. Rafael returned the next day and the king was prepared to give Rafael any of the following: one of his daughters, acres of land, a mansion with servants, bags of gold, or even half of his own kingdom, but to everyone's surprise, all Rafael asked for was one penny multiplied by two for each of the 48 squares on the chess board. All that heard Rafael's request laughed and thought that he had lost his mind. Maybe he did not understand what was being offered to him. The king made it clear to him once again that he could have anything he wanted, up to half of his kingdom, but Rafael calmly repeated his request. Therefore the king's accountant who was hysterically laughing went and retrieved the petty cash where change was held and brought a handful of pennies back. Rafael looked at the handful of pennies and said, *"You are going to need a lot more than that."* After being offered anything he wanted, all Rafael requested was one penny multiplied by 2 for every space on 64 space chessboard. Let's see how that worked out.

As they began putting the pennies on the board, those who stood by continued with their laugher and their sneers, but that laughter soon stopped as it became clear who would come out on top. As you will see, at the end of the first row, Rafael was owed $1.28; At the end of the second row, he was owed $327.68. The laugher turned to curiosity when he was owed $83,886.08 by the end of the third row. The king began sweating as he worriedly watched how the amounts quickly multiplied. The king's accountant grew visibly nervous. By the end of row 27, the King owed Rafael over 1 million dollars, but when the figure hit over 10 million dollars, the king could not contain himself anymore. Seeing how fast the amount owed was being doubled, the king begged for Rafael to release him from the offer. In exchange for the over 42 million dollars owed to Rafael, the king offered him one of his daughters, 20 acres of land, a huge mansion to sit on the land, a high position in his kingdom and a very handsome salary for the rest of his life. Rafael accepted. And to think, there were still 32 chess spaces left!

Chess Board:

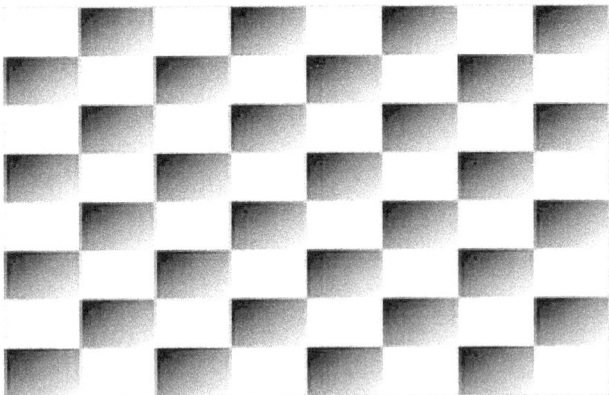

Space #1: $.01   Space #17: $1,310
Space #2: $ .04   Space #18: $2,621.44
Space #3: $.08   Space #19: $5,242.88
Space #4: $.16   Space #20: $10,485.76
Space #5: $.32   Space #21: $20,971.52
Space #6: $.64   Space #22: $41,943.04
Space #7: $1.28   Space #23: $83,886.08
Space #8: $2.56   Space #24: $167,772.16
Space #8: $5.12   Space #25: $335,544.32
Space #10: $10.24   Space #26: $671,088.64
Space #11: $20.48   Space #27: $1,342,177.28
Space #12: $40.96   Space #28: $2,684,354.56
Space #13: $81.92   Space #29: $5,368,709.12
Space #14: $163.84   Space #30: $10,737,418.24
Space #15: $327.68   Space #31: $21,474,836.48
Space #16: $655.36   Space #32: $42,949,672.96

It is important to note that the return of your money isn't this good, but this is a good illustration of how your money words. In the story of Rafael, the rate of return was 50% every year. That's is unrealistic. Nevertheless, the power of compounding works the same way based upon the rate of return. The bottom line is that the longer you leave your money invested and the higher the interest rate, the faster it will grow. However you decide to plan for retirement is up to you, but the key is to start right now. Make sure that your money is invested in plan that is making money for you. The earlier you start planning, the more financially secure you will be when it is time to retire. Be wise and start planning today.

FINANCIAL TIPS TO REMEMBER:

➢ Research has shown that those who strategically plan for the future end up with more wealth than those who do not.

➢ The first 10% of what you make should always go to you. This is called PAYING YOURSELF FIRST:

➢ A primary distinction and excellent benefit of the 401k and 403b Plans is the fact that the money invested is tax deferred, meaning that the salary deferrals are pre-taxed until you reach the age of being able to withdraw it.

➢ As of this writing (2010), an individual who is under 50 years of age may contribute a maximum of $5,000 to their Roth IRA, but the limits change from year to year.

➢ The secret that makes the rich get richer is this: If you put your money in an investment that delivers a good return and then reinvest those earnings as you receive them, the snowball effect can be astounding over the long term.

6

Taxes & Insurance

The difference between death and taxes is death doesn't get worse every time Congress meets.

~Will Rogers

*D*eath and taxes. You can try to resist them both, but at the end of it all, it is a losing proposition. In a time of economic uncertainty, knowing how to properly file your taxes can help you maximize your refund and avoid IRS audits. It is easy to learn how to file taxes if you keep good records and know the tax rules and regulations that apply to your specific situation. You must understand how income taxes work even before you get your first paycheck. When a company offers you a starting salary, you must understand how to calculate whether that salary will give you enough money after taxes to meet your financial responsibilities, goals and commitments. If you are single with no dependants and very little deductions, you will be hit much harder than someone with dependants, pre-tax deductions, mortgage interests and/or school. Having a retirement account saves and protects you significantly from getting hit hard by taxes. It is wise to make sure that all of your money is earning interest through vehicles like high-interest savings accounts, money market funds, CDs, stocks, bonds, and mutual funds. Take advantage of the tax laws. Contributing to your retirement account (401k or 403b) will result in a tax savings.

FEDERAL WITHHOLDING TAX

This is the biggest income tax that you pay to the federal government which comes directly out of your paycheck. You are required to fill out a W-4 Form when you are hired by a new employer. The information that you put on this form determines the amount of federal tax to be withheld from your future paychecks. The W-4 Form reports your marital status and the number of dependents that you claim to the IRS. Your employer collects the federal withholding tax amount and subtracts it from your income on your paycheck stub. The withholding tax monies are set aside and paid to the IRS on a quarterly basis by the company your work for. When you claim one, two, or three dependants, it means that you are financially responsible for these individuals throughout the year who are under 18 years of age. The more dependants you claim on your W4, the more money you bring home. The less number of dependants you claim, the less amount of money you will bring home and the more federal tax monies will be withheld from your check. If you are a single person with no dependants, it would be wise for you to claim zero dependants on your W4 Form. Some people claim "one" on their W4 Form for themselves in order to bring more money home in their paycheck, but the extra money is really not all that much and it is not worth it to have to pay back the IRS at the end of the year because you did not pay in enough taxes throughout the year.

The percentage you pay in income tax determines the amount of money you bring home. Some individuals have their federal tax withholding set high, so that they can get a refund during tax time. Others have it set low, in order to bring as much money home as possible. There is no one best way. Is it better to have excess money withheld and then receive a refund during tax season, or is it better to have the excess cash available in each paycheck? This question has to be answered on an individual basis, because only you know your financial situation and what is best for you. Personally, I think that it is best to overpay, rather than not pay enough and have to pay the IRS back with interest when you file your taxes. Some deliberately overpay in federal withholding so they can get a nice chunk of a refund at tax time. It is like a forced savings account to them and there is nothing like getting a lump sum of money at one time. However, other people are adamantly against this practice because excess withholding is basically an interest free loan that you are giving to the federal government. These people feel that the excess withholding could go into your Savings Account, Emergency Fund, Dream Account, IRA, or some other investment that will bring interest so that your money works for you and not the government.

FICA & MEDICARE DEDUCTION TAX

FICA is an acronym that stands for *Federal Insurance Contributions Act*. FICA tax is a percentage of money that is taken out of the paychecks of working individuals to pay Social Security Retirement and Medicare (Hospital Insurance) benefits to older Americans. It is a mandatory payroll deduction for every working individual. Two separate taxes (social security and Medicare) are added together and treated as one amount that is referred to as "payroll taxes" or FICA.

FICA tax deductions also provide benefits to widows and widowers, children who have lost their working parents, and disabled workers who qualify for benefits. The amount paid in payroll taxes throughout a person's working career is linked to the Social Security benefit that they receive as a retiree. If a working individual dies, their family may receive the social security benefits. As of this writing, FICA taxes are paid at a rate of 7.65% on gross earnings (earnings before deductions) up to $106,800 per year. The breakdown of FICA is 6.2% for Social Security and 1.45% for Medicare. FICA tax is paid by both employees and their employers. Self-employed people have to pay both halves of both taxes for a total of 15.3% of their net business earnings. These taxes are reported on Schedule SE Form with their income tax returns.

WHERE DO TAXES GO?

As you know, taxes are taken out of the paychecks of every working person and we are not always pleased about this because the federal withholding can be a big large chunk depending on the tax bracket you fall in. A person who owns a company pays their taxes either quarterly or at the end of the year, but every working individual must pay their share of taxes. It is a requirement for living in one of the freest countries in the world. Most people think that they are paying too much in taxes and often ask or wonder where their tax money goes. Well I am going to attempt to answer that for you. Taxes are typically used for public spending such as public property, institutions and services that are not privately owned, transportation, education, health, law enforcement, housing, trade and industry, overseas development and defense. State taxes, federal taxes and FICA taxes go to different places. You already learned where the FICA money goes, so below explains specifically where federal and state tax money goes.

The state taxes pays for education, police officers, firemen/women, health and social services and also government officials. Your federal dollars help to pay salaries for the senators, house of representatives and the President of the United States. Federal dollars also pay for White House employees and wars. Agriculture, foreign affairs, veteran's benefits, environmental and natural resources and interest on the national debt are also paid with federal funds.

YOUR TAX FILING STATUS

Your tax bracket depends upon two things: 1.) your taxable income and 2.) your filing status. The options for filing status are:

1. Single
2. Married Filing Jointly
3. Married Filing Separately
4. Head of Household
5. Qualifying Widow(er)

Tax rate	Single Filers	Married filing jointly or qualifying widow/widower	Married Filing Separately	Head of Household
10%	Up to $8,375	Up to $16,750	Up to $8,375	Up to $11,950
15%	$8,376 - $34,000	$16,751 - $68,000	$8,376 - $34,000	$11,951 - $45,550
25%	$34,001 - $82,400	$68,001 - $137,300	$34,001 - $68,650	$45,551 - $117,650
28%	$82,401 - $171,850	$137,301 - $209,250	$68,651 - $104,625	$117,651 - $190,550
33%	$171,851 - $373,650	$209,251 - $373,650	$104,626 - $186,825	$190,551 - $373,650
35%	$373,651 or more	$373,651 or more	$186,826 or more	$373,651 or more

The table on the previous page shows the 2010 tax brackets based upon a person's filing status. The IRS tax brackets are subject to change from year to year. Your filing status is based upon your marital and family situation on the last day of the tax year. If on the last day of the tax year, different filing statuses applied to you then you can choose one that applied during the year. Make sure that you keep copies of your income tax returns for at least seven (ideally ten) years because you will need them for various things at various times and you want to ensure that they are easily accessible so that you can get to them when you need them.

MEDICAL INSURANCE

If you are not covered under any type of medical insurance, do not wait another day to get coverage. Most major companies offer Health Benefit Plans to their employees, although the plans usually do not kick in until you have been on the job at least 90 days. However, if you are hired, at least you know that your medical insurance is forthcoming. This is another deduction that comes directly out of your check, but it is a necessity to have. Not being covered by medical insurance is dangerous. It is easier than you think to wind up in a car accident, catch a bacterial infection or trip down the stairs. Yes, there are free walk-in medical facilities that you may go to, but the quality and screenings of the medical attention you get is very low compared to individuals with adequate medical insurance. With medical coverage, you are treated noticeably different from those without it. God forbid you should come down with a debilitating disease and you need an aggressive type of medication. Without medical insurance you will not get the level of care and treatment that you would need to fight off the disease and/or infection. You can save money by getting quotes from different insurance providers to find the lowest rates. Part of being intelligent and wise, is having your life in order and this includes having medical insurance.

LIFE INSURANCE

If you have dependants, it is wise to have Life Insurance to protect their livelihood and their future. Getting sufficient life insurance could be the most important thing you ever do for your dependants. With a good life insurance benefit, you leave enough money for them to live comfortably and ultimately with sufficient money to pay for college. Even if you have no dependants right now, you should at least have a little life insurance so that if something happens to you, there will be some money to bury you. You do not want to leave a memory of you having left a financial burden on someone by them having to scrape up money to bury you. Some financial planners say that you need enough insurance to replace five to seven years of your salary. Remember, the sole purpose of life Insurance is to replace your income in case you die so that your dependents can maintain their current lifestyle.

There are two types of life insurance polices: Term insurance and Whole Life Insurance. The main difference between the two is the period of time that the insurance policy is valid, either for a short "term" or for your "whole" life. Most people buy term insurance. The price of the two types of policies also differs. Term life has a definite structure, from beginning to end for a certain number of years, which is usually from one to thirty years. Because of this structure, it usually means that term life is less expensive than whole life insurance. Whole life insurance will pay out after you die. It is inevitable that you will die eventually, but term life only pays out *if* you die within the time frame that the policy is valid. This means that the insurance company has a likelihood of taking your premium payments and never having to pay out anything on the insurance policy. It is a risk that you take. You need to know the time frame of your term policy. Another difference between whole life insurance and term life insurance is at the end of the policy, whole life policy holders have access to some of the money they paid in, whereas, at the end of a term life policy, the policy holder has absolutely nothing. This also reflects on the price difference between the two types of policies. It is understood when you take out a whole life policy that at some point, you will have access to the money that you put in. In making a decision between the two different types of policies, you should ask why you need the policy. You must review your personal situation. Do you have young children? a spouse? Consider their ages. Look at all these things before you decide on whether term or whole life insurance is better for you.

Statistics show that only two percent of term life insurance policies pay out their death benefits. Paying out a small percentage of death claims means that most of the time, term life companies just collect insurance premiums from the insured people and don't pay because the time has expired. Another point to consider is that because of the way whole life insurance policies work, the premiums go down as time progresses. However you decide is up to you, but you should definitely make sure that you do have some kind of Life Insurance.

Money solves many problems and those who have a sufficient amount of it do not have the stresses and anxiety that goes with not having enough of it. If you want financial freedom, then you must put some strategic plans in place and stick to those plans. The wealthy people of this world have patterns of thinking that the average person does not. The wealthy are smart and disciplined. They make financial sacrifices needed to make their money work for them. They make wise investments that bring in big returns. I once heard that 80% of the people in the world only make 20% of the money and 20% of the people make 80% of the money. Which side are you on? Which side do you want to be on? What do you plan on doing in order to get to the side you want to be on?

FINANCIAL TIPS TO REMEMBER:

➤ Having a retirement account saves and protects you significantly from getting hit hard by taxes.

➤ FICA is an acronym that stands for *Federal Insurance Contributions Act* and is a tax is a percentage of money that is taken out of the paychecks of working individuals to pay Social Security Retirement and Medicare (Hospital Insurance) benefits to older Americans.

➤ Your tax bracket depends upon two things: 1.) your taxable income and 2.) your filing status.

➢ Your filing status is based upon your marital and family situation on the last day of the tax year.

➢ Make sure that you keep copies of your income tax returns for at least seven (ideally ten) years because you will need them for various things at various times.

Buying Your First Home!

I always thought a yard was three feet, then I started mowing the lawn.

~*C.E. Cowman*

uying your first home is a very exciting time. It is the epitome of the American dream and one of, if not the most valuable investments you can make in your lifetime. When you get to the point in your life when you are ready to become a homeowner, you should know what to do, what to expect and how to shop. Home buying is a very intelligent and responsible decision, but it is also a step by step process. Every step must be strategically carried out before you go to the next step. You must know what to expect in terms of upfront costs, what particulars are involved in the home-buying process and the right questions to ask. Needless-to-say, your finances should already be in order. You must already know what is on your Credit Report and you should have the available upfront monies that will be required. The down payment is only one of many more costs that you will have to pay out.

This chapter is written to give you home-buying fundamentals in the most simplistic manner possible. It is written in a step by step sequential manner, so that there will be little or no misunderstandings when you are ready to shop for your home. After reading this chapter, you should be familiar with every aspect of the home-buying process and nothing should be able to blindside you. As an educated buyer, you are more likely to make good decisions and avoid pitfalls.

Home ownership is more expensive than renting when you compare all the costs involved. Unlike renting, you will be responsible for paying for repairs associated with your home as well as utility expenses. In addition to that, you will need to pay taxes and insurance. These expenses add up quickly, and if you are not financially prepared, you may end up in a large amount of debt. Even with this in mind, buying a home is one of the wisest decisions that one can make. Nothing can compare to the gratifying feeling of owning your own home. This is why your finances must be in order prior to taking the first step to homeownership. Take however long you need to get your finances in order before you purchase your first home.

There are many documents that you will need to gather and certain things that you must know prior to approaching an agent for a loan. Do your homework first. The smartest thing to do in preparation for buying your new home is to pay off as many of your bills as you can and get a copy of your Credit Report. This will help you significantly when it is time to analyze what you can afford. The up-front costs associated with home-buying can add up quickly. Most lenders require a minimum of five to twenty percent of the purchase price as a down payment. In addition to that, you must also consider the closing cost. Make sure you have enough money to cover all of these costs.

PREPARATION FOR THE PROCESS

Before we get into home buying specifics, take a look at the things that you must do in preparation for the process. Typically, you should begin preparing at least one year in advance. It could be longer depending upon the amount of money you need to save. Many home buyers are shocked when they find out that a down payment is not the only money that they need. A home inspection is a mandatory expense and can cost over $200. Closing costs may include loan origination fees, up-front "points" (prepaid interest), application fees, appraisal fees, surveys, title searches, title insurance, first month's homeowners insurance, recording fees and attorney's fees. All this will probably add up to be between 3% and 8% of your purchase price. You must be prepared for these costs. Below is a snapshot of the top three things that you will need to do in preparation for buying your home.

1. Save money for the down payment and all upfront costs.
2. Pay as many of your bills off as possible, especially the ones with high balances.
3. Review your Credit Report and correct any errors on it.

Before you begin looking at houses, you must know the price range that you can afford. By calculating how much house you can afford, you will have a better idea of where to begin. For example, if you can afford a maximum monthly payment of $1,000, you will be looking at a total mortgage of $166,792 (assuming a 30-year fixed rate at six percent). Knowing this limit will help you to be realistic and keep you from getting too attached to a home listed at $250,000.

1) **PREQUALIFICATION** (optional)
Prequalification helps you focus on homes you can afford. A prequalification is when a professional gives you an estimate of how much money you "may" be able to borrow based upon your gross income and amount of debt. Since prequalification is only an "estimate", you should not have to complete an application or provide documentation, nor should you pay anything. A pre-

qualification is nothing more than a snapshot based upon your current financial situation. It really does not carry any weight other than giving you an idea of how much of a mortgage loan you may quality for.

2) **GET PRE-APPROVED** (mandatory)
   This is the first "official" step to owning your own home. You have to shop for a loan and in order to do this, you must get a pre-approval. Different financial institutions give mortgage loans such as credit unions, banks, pension funds, insurance companies and finance companies. Some people go directly to the bank where they have their checking and savings account to inquire about a mortgage loan. Know before hand where you will go to shop for your two mortgage quotes. You will complete an application wherever you go for a pre-approval, but you are never obligated to accept any offer. However, you may pay for each of them to pull your Credit Report. It is a good idea to shop around for the best rates because terms and options do vary. Unless you shop around, you will almost certainly pay too much in interest rates. This can cost you *tens of thousands of dollars* over the life of your loan, so choose the lowest rate and be wise.

   Out of all the institutions that lend money, Mortgage Brokers are the only ones who *specialize* in the area of finding home loans. Brokers know the market and can be a valuable source of information concerning the home buying process. They do not work for any one specific lending institution, but they do work with dozens of different lenders. Their main job is to find lenders with the terms and rates that are best for the buyer. Brokers oftentimes get special wholesale rates from lenders as well. It is wise to get a minimum of two loan estimates and choose the one with the lowest interest rate and ideally no points. Statistics report that up to 85% of borrowers pay an interest rate that is too high. Once your Credit Report is pulled and reviewed, the broker or agent will be able to tell you how much lenders are willing to loan you and under what circumstances.

Full disclosure of your finances is required in order to get an accurate depiction of how much you quality for. Always be honest when completing the process. Do not let anyone persuade you to make a false statement on your loan application, such as overstating your income, the source of your down payment, failing to disclose the nature and amount of your debts, or even how long you have been employed. When you apply for a mortgage loan, every piece of information that you submit must be accurate and complete. Lenders want to make sure that you will be able to pay back the loan. This is why your credit should be as clean as it could be. You should have paid down as many of your bills as possible and should already know what is on your Credit Report. Be ready to answer certain questions about what may be on it. Pre-approval does not guarantee you a loan, but it does mean that the lender may commit to giving you a loan if you meet certain requirements and if the home you plan on buying meets certain conditions. During the pre-approval process, you will need to certain documents and if you know what they are now, you can begin gathering them together to bring with you when you go to meet with the broker (or other agent) for the pre-approval. These documents include, but are not limited to:

- ✓ Your last four paycheck stubs
- ✓ Six months worth of bank statements from all bank accounts you have
- ✓ Three years worth of tax returns

- ✓ Proof of any additional income (child support, etc)
- ✓ Proof of how you will make the down payment
- ✓ Written explanations for any late payments you may have on your Credit Report
- ✓ Written explanations for any charge offs, repossessions, evictions or other derogatory entries on your credit report.

Credit is always an issue. Good credit with high FICO scores means that you will get favorable terms on your loan. Bad credit might prevent you from getting any loan. Lenders who specialize in making loans to buyers with bad credit are known as predatory lenders who give subprime mortgages. More information on this is given later in this chapter.

THE GOOD FAITH ESTIMATE (GFE)

The Good Faith Estimate referred to as a GFE is just that - an estimate and must be provided within three business days of applying for a loan. It is a standard form which is intended to be used to compare different offers from different lenders or brokers. It includes an itemized list of fees and costs associated with your loan estimate. In the United States, the GFE must be provided to a customer by a mortgage lender or broker. This is required by the Real Estate Settlement Procedures Act (RESPA).

When you receive your GFE, be sure to review it very carefully because the lender directly controls many of the fees on it, and those are the ones that you must pay the most attention to when comparing loan offers. Ask questions if you don't understand something. Some fees are generated by third parties, which you have no control over. When comparing GFEs, those third party fees should be pretty similar in price. Other fees are under your control and can be adjusted, particularly, the ones that the lender tacks on. Additionally, there are taxes and government fees that should be the same across the board regardless of the lender. A GFE shows your interest rate and any discount points that you can pay at closing. Make sure you understand that paying discount points will buy you a lower interest rate and will lower your monthly payments, but it will take a while before the savings will make up for the fee. The point fees also must be paid then and there and can be as high as 4 points ($4,000). Smart shoppers obtain good-faith estimates from two or more lenders, compare their costs and ask questions about any large discrepancies.

Lenders follow two rules of thumb to determine how much you can afford to pay and your pre-approval may go through with certain "conditions." These conditions will need to be satisfied as soon as possible.

Rule #1:
Your mortgage payment should not be more than 32% of your gross monthly income. Mortgage payments normally include principal, interest, taxes and insurance also known as P.I.T.I. for short. What lenders do is add up your housing expenses to determine what percentage they are of your gross monthly income. This figure is known as your Gross Debt Service (GDS) ratio. Remember, it has to be 32% or less of your gross household monthly income.

Rule #2:
Your entire monthly debt load should not be more than 40% of your gross monthly income. This includes debts such as car payment(s), credit card payments or other loans. Lenders add up these debts to determine what percentage they are of your gross household monthly income. This figure is called your Total Debt Service (TDS) ratio.

The amount of house you can afford to buy depends on the terms of your mortgage and the interest rate. The term is the total length of time over which payments will be paid. This is normally 15 or 30 years. The rate can be fixed (never changes) or adjustable (fluctuates). Thirty-year fixed-rate mortgages are considered conventional and are the most popular. The longer the term the lower your monthly payment will be and a fixed rate provides stability over the life of your loan. The drawbacks are low principal payments in the early years and the risk that market rates will decline over the term. However, if your credit history is pretty good and you have sufficient income, you can usually refinance your mortgage for a better interest rate when rates decline and get lower than what you pay.

A 15-year term lowers your interest rate, reduces total interest payments and increases principal payments. But it also increases your monthly payment. If you can not afford the higher payments at the time of your loan, a 30-year mortgage may be more feasible for you. If there are no prepayment penalties, you can always make additional principal payments as your income increases. Making just one extra monthly payment a year will pay off your 30-year mortgage in less than 22 years and will save tens of thousands of dollars in interest costs.

If you do not plan on staying in your home more than three years, you might benefit from an adjustable-rate mortgage (ARM). Adjustable-rate Mortgages offer initial rates that are lower than fixed mortgages. At some point, however, usually after the first year, the rates are tied to market conditions and are subject to rate increases. Most ARMs have a cap on rate increases in any given year, as well as over the life of the loan. Some ARMs offer initial rates at least 2% below fixed rates and limit increases to 1% annually and 5% to 6% over the life of the loan. Many home buyers are attracted by the affordability of an ARM during the initial period, but you must have the money to be able to afford the monthly payment when it increases and sometimes it increases double or even triple what you are used to paying.

DIFFERENT TYPES OF MORTGAGE LOANS

For the most part, there are three different kinds of loans (Conventional, FHA, and VA loans). It is your lender's job to find the best loan for your needs and qualifications. Since you will hear these terms frequently, it is not a bad thing to know what they mean.

Conventional. This is just a regular, standard loan that does not exceed 80% of the value of the home and is either fixed or adjustable. Your down payment is typically 20% of the purchase price of the house or market value. If you pay less than 20% as a down payment, you will need a high-ratio mortgage. This type of mortgage usually requires mortgage insurance. Your lender may add the mortgage insurance premium to your mortgage or ask you to pay it in full at closing. A conventional mortgage is a type of mortgage in which the terms and conditions of the loan meet the criteria set forth by Fannie Mae and Freddie Mac.

Federal Housing Association (FHA). The U.S. government offers this program to make home-buying easier. The FHA loan is a partially guaranteed loan, which makes it easier for banks to give. Through the FHA Loan, the government guarantees part of your loan to the bank, so if you default, FHA will pay the bank back if you fail to make your payments. FHA will only pay the bank *after* your house has been foreclosed on. There is a little more red tape involved in order to get an FHA loan and the house has to be in excellent condition in order to pass an FHA inspection, but in the long run, it is better for you because you know you are getting a good house. A financial advantage of an FHA loan is that they only require 3.5% down.

But of course, the more a buyer puts down, the lower the monthly mortgage payment will be. Low mortgage balances carry low mortgage payments.

Veteran Affairs Loans (VA). This type of loan is only offered to veterans and it is not uncommon for them not to put a penny down. As with FHA loans, the VA guarantees part of the loan to the bank if the homeowner defaults, which makes lenders feel comfortable lending the money. The three types of loans, Conventional, FHA, and VA are the most common types of loans given to buy homes. You must question if you are getting some other kind of loan. Check figures and fees and always ask questions.

By getting pre-approved, you will know exactly how much you will be able to borrow for your new home and what kind of loan you qualify for. It is always better to get the pre-approval before you make an offer on a home. You will get the pre-approval based upon your income, credit history, and amount of debt you already owe. This helps you to look for a home within your price range. Once all of your documents have been reviewed and any required conditions have been met, the lender will offer you the option of locking in your interest rate. If you know you are getting a good rate and you are comfortable with the monthly house payment, then lock it in right away.

WHICH TYPE OF MORTGAGE IS BEST?

Fixed-rate Mortgages. As mentioned earlier, this is a mortgage in which the interest rate does not change during the entire life of the loan. Most fixed-rate loans are amortized for a certain period of time, meaning if the borrower makes the principal and interest payment every month over the term as agreed, the loan will be paid in full at the end of that time. If you take out a fixed rate loan when rates are low, the fixed rate would enable you to lock in the low rates and not be concerned with fluctuations as in an ARM. On the other hand, if interest rates are high at the time of your loan, you may benefit from a ARM because as the prime rate falls to low or normal levels, the rate on the loan would decrease. If you are told that your loan is fixed, check to see how long it will remain fixed. Unless it is 15 or 30 years or more, you have some type of adjustable-rate mortgage, or ARM.

Adjustable-rate Mortgage (ARM). An Adjustable Rate Mortgage (ARM) has an interest rate that is fixed for the first several years of the loan (typically 3, 5, or 7 years) then goes up or down for the remainder of the loan based on market conditions. The interest rate in the early years of an ARM is usually much lower than that of a conventional fixed rate 30 year mortgage, which makes an ARM more affordable for people whose incomes are lower now than they expect it to be in a few years. An ARM can also be advantageous for a homeowner who expects to move to a larger home in less than 10 years. With an ARM, the interest rate can increase or decrease depending on the index and margin agreed upon. Some ARMs allow the homeowner to convert to a fixed-rate loan at some point down the line. This is a valuable feature and borrowers typically have to pay extra for it. Ask your loan officer whether your loan has this feature.

An ARM has four components: (1) an index, (2) a margin, (3) an interest rate cap structure, and (4) an initial interest rate period. When the initial interest rate period has ended, the new interest rate is calculated by adding the margin to the index. Your lender should tell you what the margin is at the time of the Loan Application (margins may vary from lender to lender, so it is a good idea to shop around for a low margin if you go this route). As the index figure moves up or down, your interest rate will be adjusted.

Interest-only Mortgages. Interest-only mortgage payments are made up of interest only and do not include any principal.

When the loan is due, the original balance is still due. The cost for an interest-only mortgage is a bit higher than a conventional loan. For example, if a 30-year fixed-rate mortgage is available at the going rate of 6% interest, an interest-only mortgage might cost an extra 1/2 percent or be set at 6.5%. A lender might also charge a percentage of a point to originate the loan. All lender fees vary, so it pays to shop around. The important aspect of an interest-only mortgage is that the loan balance will never increase. The risk associated with an interest-only mortgage lies in being forced to sell the property if the property has not gone up in value. When a home owner only pays the interest each month, then at the end of five years, the balance owed on the mortgage will still be the same amount it was on the first day of the closing because no money was paid on the principal.

The most popular interest-only mortgages does not allow borrowers to make an interest-only payment forever. Generally, that time period is limited to the first five or ten years of the loan. After that period, the loan is amortized for the remainder of its term. This means the payments move up to an amortized amount, but the loan balance is not increased. The most two popular interest only mortgages are the following:

A 30-year Interest Only Mortgage. The option to make interest-only payments is for the first 60 months (five years). On a $200,000 loan at 6.5%, the borrower has the option to pay $1,083 per month at any time within the first five years. For years 6 through 30, the payment will be $1,264, which includes both interest and principle.

A 40-year Interest Only Mortgage. The option to make interest-only payments is for the first 120 months (ten years). On a $200,000 loan at 6.5%, the borrower has the option for the first ten years to pay an interest-only payment in any given month. For years 11 through 40, the payment will be $1,264, which includes both interest and principle.

Negative-amortization Mortgage. Negative amortization occurs when the monthly payment is less than full interest and does not pay any principal. The interest that is unpaid accrues and the principle balance owed increases. This is NEVER a good loan to get.

PREDATORY LENDING

Your history of good credit works for you in a wonderful way when you are shopping for a mortgage loan. Good credit will save you literally hundreds of thousand of dollars in APR fees and interest rates that people with bad credit are not privy to. On the other hand, if you have a history of not paying your bills on time and your credit is not very good or down right poor, you may still get a mortgage, but you are predisposed to predatory lenders who give subprime mortgages if you are not careful.

As a first-time uneducated, misinformed home-buyer, with bad credit, you are a prime candidate for becoming a victim of Predatory Lending. Look at the word "predatory". It is derived from the word *"predator"* which means, *one who searches for prey in order to take advantage of them*. Predatory lenders typically steer borrowers into subprime mortgages even sometimes when the borrowers could qualify for a conventional loan. A Predatory Lender benefits substantially by offering a home loan or persuading someone into refinancing their home with outlandish and unscrupulous terms. Predatory Lenders entice, induce and/or assist borrowers in taking out "subprime" mortgages that carry high fees, high interest rates, strips the borrower of equity in their home, or places the borrower in a lower credit rating status in order to benefit the subprime lender. Wherever there are a large percentage of low-income homeowners or other groups of individuals who are financially vulnerable, such as the elderly, there is the possibility of greedy mortgage companies or con-artists approaching these individuals and taking advantage of them. According to a government study, over half (51%) of refinance mortgages in predominantly African-American neighborhoods are subprime loans, compared to only 9% of refinances in predominantly white neighborhoods. While the actions of these "predators" are not always illegal, the result can still be devastating for the homeowners and may cause them to ultimately lose their home while the "professionals" who supposedly "helped" them are the only ones who end up profiting. Predatory lending practices can leave victims homeless and defeated, stripped of self-respect and hope and leave their credit ruined.

Each situation of Predatory Lending takes unfair advantage of a homeowner's financial needs by charging unconscionable fees and charges. Buying and/or refinancing your home may be one of the most important and complex financial decisions you will ever make. There are many lenders, Mortgage Brokers, appraisers, and/or real estate professionals who are sincerely and honestly ready to help people acquire their American Dream of owning their own home or refinancing their current home and get a fair loan while doing it. However, you need to understand the home buying process in order to be a smart consumer. Every year, misinformed homebuyers, often first-time purchasers or senior citizens, become victims of predatory lending or loan fraud. This is why the application of knowledge is power!

SUBPRIME MORTGAGES

A subprime mortgage is a type of loan offered to people with very poor credit scores (often below 600). Because of their low scores, these people usually do not qualify for a conventional mortgage loan. Since they pose a very high risk for defaulting on their loans due to poor payment history, the interest rates that they are given are enormously high. A sub-prime lender is one who makes the loans to these people. A sub-prime lender will never identify themselves as such. It would be too obvious. The only indication you have that you may be dealing with a Subprime Lender is the astronomical costs of the fees and the extremely high percentage and interest rates, which are ridiculously higher than those of conventional rates. What is sad is that borrowers who sometimes qualify for regular financing are sometimes induced to borrow from a Subprime Lender. Over 95% of Subprime mortgages have a very steep pre-payment penalty. In fact, about 70% of subprime mortgages have prepayment penalties, compared with about 2% of conventional loans.

NOTHING GOOD IN PREDATORY LENDING!

Predatory Lending drains money from families, destroys the pride of homeownership, and often leads to foreclosure. It is estimated that predatory mortgage lending costs Americans more than $9.1 billion each year. Below are some of the characteristics of predatory lending. It is good to know what they are so you can run in the opposite direction when you see them or anything remotely close to them.

Excessive Fees:
A refinanced or subprime mortgage is usually packed with excessive unnecessary fees. Regular mortgages usually have loan fees below 1% of the total amount of the loan. A predatory mortgage can have loan fees in excess of 5%. These excessive costs are disguised into the loan amount so they are not easily recognizable. These fees put thousands of dollars into the predator's pockets at the homeowner's expense. On conventional loans, fees below 1% of the loan amount are common. On predatory loans, fees totaling more than 5% of the loan amount are common.

Prepayment Penalty: Over 80% of subprime mortgages have a prepayment penalty. An abusive prepayment penalty costs more than six month's interest. In the prime market, about 2%

of home loans have prepayment penalties, but in the subprime market, the prepayment penalties are as high as five percent. This makes refinancing very hard for the victim of a subprime loan to do.

Tax Refund Anticipation Loans (RALs):
These are short-term cash advances that are given in expectation of a customer's tax refund. But, the loans are offered at very high interest rates, ranging from 40% to over 70% APR! Also, they speed up the refund process by as little as one week, compared to what consumers usually can expect by filing online.

Insurance and Other Unnecessary Products:
Predators often add insurance and other unnecessary things to the loan amount. The insurance can include fire and hazard insurance, regular mortgage insurance, disability insurance, life insurance, homeowner's insurance and even health insurance. The premium for these is also added to the loan amount where the cost is not easily noticed by the borrower. The predator earns large commissions every year on the premiums paid.

Abusive and Abnormal Prepayment Penalties:
The prepayment penalty is an astronomical fee that the lender requires the borrower to pay if the house is paid off early. The home owner usually has less-than-perfect credit when originally taking out the mortgage and the prepayment penalty is typically hidden in the fine print. Over the next few years, a homeowner may improve their credit and want to obtain a new mortgage with lower interest rates. However, the prepayment penalty on the original mortgage (which often equals 5% of the original loan) is so high that it eats up any equity built up and can even leave them owing more money. Homeowners often have no choice other than to keep the original, high-interest mortgage. This is also another case where the lender gives a *kickback* to the mortgage broker for helping to include the high

prepayment penalty in the mortgage terms. In the future, when the homeowner has to pay the prepayment penalty, the mortgage broker pockets more money.

Loan Flipping:
Another form of predatory lending practices occurs when con-artists finds a homeowner who they can talk or coerce into refinancing their mortgage, even though the homeowner gains nothing from the transaction. This is called *loan flipping*. While the transaction might put some money into the homeowner's bank account, this amount is easily eaten up by excessive fees, higher interest rate, and prepayment penalties of the new mortgage. A serious danger with loan flipping occurs when a *balloon payment* is inserted into the fine print. While the homeowners originally may have had twenty or thirty years to pay on the mortgage, under loan flipping they might be signing for a two, three, or five year balloon payment. At the end of that time they need to find a way to refinance the house again or lose it completely. Of course, the con-artists will be glad to do another *loan flip* and refinance it for them once again pocketing thousands of dollars in the process and leaving the homeowner with even less equity in the property than before.

Mandatory Arbitration:
Another practice that falls within the definition of predatory lending happens when a lender hides words in the fine print that make it illegal for the homeowner to take legal action against the lender. The *borrowers sign away their rights to sue the lender for any fraud, predatory actions or illegal actions*. The only right the borrowers have is to take their grievances to arbitration. The arbitration process is totally in the hands of the lenders and is usually conducted in secret without the home owner having any representation. Although the borrowers can usually have legal counsel, they find it difficult to find anyone who will represent them because the lawyers are not

guaranteed payment of their fees in arbitration like they are in court. Many arbitration cases are handled over the phone and when a small individual is fighting against a large corporation and the proceedings are confidential with no written record of the facts, the borrower is at a disadvantage. Most arbitration decisions are binding and the borrowers cannot appeal them. Mandatory arbitration makes it much less likely that borrowers will receive fair and appropriate treatment in cases of wrongdoing.

More than 50% of the lenders are now including mandatory arbitration in their loan documents and the borrowers remain unaware of this. Lenders favor arbitration because it eliminates the right of a homeowner to do a class-action suit against the lender. The Fair Credit Reporting Act and the Truth in Lending Act have no bearing in an arbitration situation, only if one can go to court. And, some lenders keep their right to go to court but prohibit the borrower from doing so. The fees for arbitration can also be more expensive than filing a small claims court suit. Overall, the borrowers who sign a mandatory arbitration contract are bound to a very lopsided arrangement that is not in their best interest. The major arbitration administrators that a borrower can utilize are the National Arbitration Forum, the American Arbitration Association (ADR), and Jams Endispute.

GOOD NEWS!

Predatory lending laws are slowly being fought against in the legal systems of the federal government and individual states. More than 35 states have already placed a legal limit on the maximum prepayment penalty that a homeowner should have to pay, and over half of the states have taken steps to limit predatory lending practices.

More and more homeowners are becoming aware that they have the right to report mortgage fraud and predatory lending. Policy makers, consumer advocates and civil rights leaders are taking stronger action against the con-artists who specialize in predatory lending practices. With this awareness in place, the elderly, the minorities and those with less income are less likely to be prey for predators. Politicians on every level are becoming more aware of the need for predatory lending laws. Organizations like the Center for Responsible Lending, the National Association of Mortgage Brokers, the Mortgage Bankers Association (MBA) and the American Bar Association actively work to promote predatory lending laws. They also know that educating the public is one of the strongest deterrents to mortgage fraud and predatory lending practices. These organizations are committed to providing this education.

ANNUAL PERCENTAGE RATES

APR stands for Annual Percentage Rate and has to do with how much money you will be paying upfront in order to get the best rate for your loan. It is nothing more than an *estimate* of the various costs of your loan, including the interest rate. It is not exact to the number, since some of the figures will vary between the time of calculation and the time of closing. There can be differences in the costs included in a mortgage APR. The *Federal Truth in Lending Law* requires mortgage companies to list the APR of their loans when they advertise an interest rate. This prevents them from advertising unduly low interest rates and then tacking on fees and other costs that drive up the real cost of the loan. All fees are calculated over the life of the loan, which means that if a loan is repaid early through refinancing or other means, the initial APR figure is not correct. The APR presumes that people keep their loans for their duration, which does not always happen that way.

The APR does not take into account certain charges, such as loan origination fees, which the lender charges to process the loan, private mortgage insurance, application fees, credit check fees, title insurance premiums, fees for title examination, property appraisals and document preparation.

Another charge that is often included is discount points, which are upfront payments that lower the interest rate. The APR does not have to be perfectly accurate. The lender may round up or down to the nearest one-eighth of a percentage point. The mortgage APR can come in different forms. An *Effective APR* looks at the simple interest generated in one year. The *Nominal APR* evaluates compound interest in one year and is more accurate. As a borrower, you should ask whether you are being shown effective or nominal rates. A shorter loan may have a higher APR because it has fewer total months in which to spread all fees. However, this does not necessarily mean that you will save money with a longer duration loan with a lower APR.

The APR takes into consideration fees and costs including:

Discount Points

Points are additional up-front fees, paid in lieu of higher interest rates. When your money is low, lenders usually charge points, also known as Loan Origination Fees. Each "point" is equal to 1 percent of the loan amount. Therefore, 2 points on a $100,000 loan will cost $2,000. The higher the cost of the home, the more expensive the points are. Points buy down your interest rate, meaning the more points you pay, the lower your interest rate will be. Points are tax deductible. If points are not required and you elect to pay off points to lower your interest rate, it will not be included in your APR. However, if you are required to pay off points, this cost will be factored in when your APR is calculated.

Origination Fees

Often confused with points, this is a fee the lender charges for the work they perform on your behalf, also known as processing fees. Basically, it is the same as the labor that you pay when someone works on your car.

Mortgage Insurance Premiums

This is insurance that you pay against defaulting on payment of your loan. Your lender may require you to pay mortgage insurance if your down payment is less than 20 percent of what you pay for the home.

Prepaid Mortgage Interest

Since interest is paid on a monthly basis and is included in your mortgage payment, prepaid mortgage interest is paid at closing to cover the gap between the time you close and the first of the next month.

To explain how the APR can be used for comparison purposes, below is an example of a simple APR:

You are shopping for a 30-year mortgage for $100,000.

Bank #1 offers you a 30-year fixed mortgage at a six percent interest rate.

Bank #2 offers you a 30-year fixed mortgage at a 5 percent interest rate.

Your first instinct would be to go with Bank #2 because of the lower interest rate. However, Bank #2 charges a $2,000 Origination Fee (the fee to process the loan), and you are required to pay four points, which is $4,000 on your $100,000 loan. Bank #1 has no Origination Fee and requires you to pay no points. Suddenly you will be paying $6,000 more if you go with bank #2. The APR will factor this into the overall equation and Bank #1 will have the lower, and potentially more attractive APR. These are things that most people do not know and therefore do not know what to look for or what questions to ask. Once all of these financial logistics are taken care of and you are clear on the terms of your new loan, the fun part begins - house shopping.

3) **HOUSE SHOPPING**. *Choosing a Neighborhood*

In searching for a home, the best thing to do is first find the neighborhood or development that you would like to live in. Different people have different things they look for when trying to find the right home. For those who have children, schools play a significant role because of the quality of education their children will be getting. Crime rates, gated communities, transportation accessibility and closeness to family and friends may be things to consider. You would also need to be sure that you are not buying a home that is in a flood zone. If so, your property value would be less inclined to go up in that neighborhood. Some people want to live close to their job. Some want to be close to their families. All these factors depend on you as the buyer and what is important to you. Some people do not mind the long drive to work. I will advise you however, to look for a neighborhood where prices are increasing. As the prices of the better homes increase, values of the lesser homes in the area may increase as well. If you find a less expensive home in a good neighborhood, make sure you factor in the cost of repairs or upgrades that such a home may need.

You must know what you want. How many bedrooms and bathrooms would you like? Do you want a one or two story home? Would you prefer a town home, condominium or single family home? A gated community or open neighborhood? Do you want a pool? an office? a family room? a garage? All of these things must be taken into consideration when you are shopping for your new home. You will inform your real estate agent of your home requirement desires and he or she will do a search on the ones that meet your criteria.

YOUR REAL ESTATE AGENT

No one will play a more important role in helping you find a home than your Real Estate Agent. Your Real Estate

Agent's job is to provide you with pertinent information about homes for sale and take you out to look at houses. Based on the information you give on the kind of home you want, your Real Estate Agent will search the Multiple Listing System (MLS) and identify homes that meet your needs and price range. My suggestion is to look for houses that are a little over your price range so that you can have room to negotiate the price down. For instance, if you have been pre-approved for a $225,000 home, you can search for homes in the $226,000 -$245,000 price range and talk the price down. Your realtor gives you guidance about how much to offer.

It is important to keep in mind that the realtor has an incentive when the price is higher because the higher the price of the house is, the more of a commission they get. An honest realtor will make decisions based upon the best interest of the buyer, not his or her own financial interests. Not everyone uses a realtor. Some individuals find their own homes. However, this can take a lot of time if you do not have access to the MLS and must drive around to find homes for sale yourself. Some potential home buyers have already identified the house they want. If this is the case, then you do not need a realtor! Cut the middle man out and use the money that would be paid to a realtor as commission to your advantage. When there is no realtor, there is greater opportunity of talking the price of the house down because the seller does not have that 3% commission to pay to the realtor, so if the asking price of the house is $230,000, you have a 3% window of negotiation. If the seller goes down the full 3% then you come out on top. You end up paying $223,100 for a $230,000 home, saving a total discount of $6,900. Without having to pay a realtor, the seller is more inclined to go down on the price of the house. As a buyer, you must also keep in mind that there are houses that are "for sale by owner". These are homes that sellers are trying to sell on their own without the help of an agent. These homes are not listed in the MLS. Therefore, realtors do not have access to them. If a buyer finds a "for sale by owner" home themselves, they really do not need a realtor. If you have found that home on your own, why do you need a realtor? Some people do find their own home, but still use their real-estate agent to help with negotiations and drawing up the contract, so it really is up to the buyer whether or not they feel a realtor is necessary.

Another very important question to ask is the cost of property taxes on the home you are thinking about buying. Before you have a contract drawn, find out what the property taxes are. Do your own homework so that you can compare the taxes of the home you are interested in with the homes in that neighborhood. This is extremely important because it could make the difference in the amount of your monthly payment. When I was looking for my second home, I found a very nice house for sale. The cost was perfect for me and the house was in a clean, quiet neighborhood. It was a house for sale that I happened to see while taking a different route home from work. I immediately called my mortgage broker, who was also a certified realtor. He had access to the MLS and we had been searching for and going by homes that met my criteria. He was such a knowledgeable person and had my best interest at heart. He was honest, had integrity and was my guardian angel throughout my home-buying process. I gave him the property address and told him that I really liked that house and desired to see the inside. I wasn't even home ten minutes when he called and informed me that the property taxes on that house were $10,000! The home was a single story three bedroom two-bath. The average property taxes of the homes on that same street and surrounding streets were around $1,700. I asked him why the taxes on that particular house were so high and he informed me that I would be the fifth family to live there. Apparently, the more a home is bought and sold, the higher the property taxes are. That was certainly an eye-opening learning experience for me, so I am sharing it with you as well. I am not so sure that real-estate agents or lenders will give you this information, but it is very important. An extra

$10,000 will make a huge difference in your mortgage payment. This is why you need to ask how much the property taxes are on the home you choose. Well, to end the story, I ended up getting an even bigger home – a two story, four bedroom, four bathroom, with a two-car garage and an office for just a little more than the one story, three bedroom that I liked; and the property taxes of the home I bought? $2,500! I was the second owner. What a big difference. It doesn't seem to make sense but that is the way it is.

4) MAKE AN OFFER

Once you find the perfect home for you and have done the background search on the home, you will make an offer. If the seller accepts your offer, a contract will be drawn up and both of you will sign it. If the seller does not agree to your offer, they may come back with a counter-offer or vice versa. The process repeats until an agreement is reached. Once the contract is signed by both parties, it becomes officially binding.

When you and your realtor determine what conditions will be in the contract, be sure to insist that the contract states that the offer is *"contingent upon a home inspection"* conducted by a qualified inspector. You as the buyer will have to pay for the inspection yourself, but it could keep you from buying a house that will cost you far more in repairs down the road.

5) PAY YOUR DEPOSIT

This is part of your down payment and must be paid when you make an offer to purchase. The cost varies, but it may be up to 5% of the purchase price. If you give a deposit of 5%, then your down payment is considered to be made. Remember that if you are getting a conventional mortgage, you are typically expected to pay up to 20% of the cost of the home, so you still must have the other 15% ready to pay at closing.

6) GET A HOME INSPECTION

After you have signed the contract, you are ready to proceed to the next step, which is getting a Home Inspection. The inspector will go through the property and perform a comprehensive visual inspection to assess the condition of the house and all of its systems. He or she will look for hidden problems with the home such as structural, electrical, wiring, water damage, etc. Every inspection should include a visual assessment of at least the following: the foundation of the home, all doors and windows, the roof and exterior walls, the attic, plumbing and electrical systems (where visible), heating and air conditioning systems, ceilings, walls and floors, mold problems, termites, ventilation, septic tanks, wells or sewer lines and any other buildings such as a detached garage, the lot, and/or drainage away from buildings. After the inspection is conducted, you will get an overall evaluation of the structural integrity of your potential new home. The report will reveal if something is not functioning properly, needs to be changed or is unsafe. After reviewing the report, you may discover concerns that may warrant withdrawing your offer to purchase the home or discuss how the required repairs may affect the sale price that was agreed upon. The home inspector does not estimate the value of the house. That is what an appraiser does. If you are satisfied with the results of the inspection, then proceed with the process.

7) GET A PROPERTY APPRAISAL

An appraisal is an estimate of the actual value of the home by a neutral third party at the time you are trying to purchase. It helps to ensure that you are not paying too much for the home. The appraisal should include an unbiased assessment of the property's physical and functional characteristics, an analysis of recent comparable sales in that neighborhood and an assessment of current market conditions affecting the property. Most lenders require appraisals on properties prior to loan approvals to ensure that the mortgage loan amount is not more than the value of the property. Appraisals are mainly for lenders. Home inspections are mainly for buyers.

8) GOING INTO ESCROW

After you have signed a contract on a home, your lender will require you to open an Escrow Account to cover insurance and taxes. Money put in an escrow account is held by a neutral third party called an Escrow Agent who is someone from a title company or an escrow company. The job of the Agent is to carry out the pre-determined instructions agreed upon by all involved parties (buyer, seller, and lender) upon completion of terms and conditions. The money and/or documents in the Escrow Account are released when all terms of the agreement are met. The rationale behind having this account is to protect the lender by ensuring that you pay your taxes and insurance on time. When an Escrow Account is opened, you will keep it throughout the term of your loan. In the beginning, you will make an initial deposit, followed by payments into the account every month. This money normally comes out of your regular mortgage payment. Escrow monies benefit borrowers by helping them spread insurance and tax expenses evenly over 12 payments. Once everything for escrow is completed during the home-buying process, you will sign the closing papers.

9) CLOSING DAY!

The Closing Agent will inform all relevant parties of the date, time, and place of where the closing will be held. It is usually at an attorney's office or at the escrow company. This is the big day, the day that the house officially becomes yours! To close means to "close" the deal on the contract made between you and the seller to buy the home. At closing, the transfer of ownership of the house from the seller to you will officially be made and all monies owed will be paid during this time. You will be asked to sign many documents and affidavits during closing. Joining you around the table at this Closing Meeting will typically be you, the seller, possibly an attorney, your Real

Estate Agent (if used), and the Closing Agent. Your lender may also attend. It is the Closing Agent who will conduct the meeting. On the day of closing, you must present the Homeowner's Insurance Policy. The seller will present proof that specified repairs were made (if applicable), bring warranties and/or other relevant documents pertaining to the home. Other documents specific to the transaction may also be brought.

You are allowed to review the closing documents presented to you before paying the total amount due and before signing everything. Read everything carefully and ask questions if you have to. Do not sign anything that you do not understand. If you cannot afford an attorney, take your documents to a HUD-approved housing counseling agency in your area to find out if they will review the documents for you or can refer you to an attorney who will help you for free or at a low cost. If you have an attorney present with you, there is nothing wrong with asking for the closing documents in advance so that your attorney can go through them with you beforehand. You should take time to read all the documents and understand them fully. Never sign a blank document or a document that has blanks in it. If information is inserted by someone else *after* you have signed it, you may still be bound to the terms of the contract. If you see blanks on a document, then write "N/A" (i.e., not applicable) on the line or cross through any blanks. Also make sure that the correct title is on the deed. Additionally, before signing your name to any documents, be sure that the interest rates, miscellaneous fees and the condition of the property are all what you agreed to. Honest mistakes have been known to happen and those mistakes can be costly for you and harder to correct down the line – especially if you have already signed your name to them.

As a buyer, you will receive a copy of the following documents on the day of closing:

Mortgage Note: The mortgage note represents a promise to pay the lender according to the agreed terms. The terms of the loan are set forth, including the date on which the payments must be made each month and the address to where they must be sent. The note also explains the penalties that will be assessed if you default on your loan and warns you that the mortgage lender can "call" the loan (require full repayment before the end of the loan term) if you fail to make the required payments.

Title or Deed: The seller must bring the deed to the closing, properly signed and notarized. It is the document that transfers ownership from them to you.

Settlement Statement: This form, required by federal law, itemizes the services provided and lists the charges to the buyer and the seller. It is filled out by the Closing Agent who conducts the closing. Both the buyer and seller must sign it.

Certificate of Occupancy: If you are buying a newly constructed house, you need this legal document to move in.

Once all documents have been signed by all involved parties and all monies are paid, the keys are finally handed over to you. The deed indicating you as a new homeowner will be recorded in the State Registry of Deeds. The legal transfer of the property usually takes one to two days after closing. If at all possible, avoid closing on a Friday, at the end of the month or before long weekends. If anything goes wrong, the banks and/or other needed businesses will be closed. The Closing Agent usually will not release the check to the seller or the real-estate agent until the transaction has been recorded.

You will probably have to pay the interest on the mortgage from the date of settlement to the beginning of the period covered by the first monthly payment. For example, suppose you settle on March 10th. Your first monthly payment begins to accrue on April 1 and will be payable at the beginning of May. At closing you may be required to prepay the interest for the period from March 10 through the end of March. This means that if you settle later in the month, your closing costs will be less than if you settle early in the month.

TAX BENEFITS OF HOME OWNERSHIP

As long as your mortgage balance is smaller than the price of your home, the interest you pay is fully deductible on your tax return unless the home is more than one million dollars. If you are the proud owner of a multimillion-dollar mansion, the Internal Revenue Service (IRS) will limit your deductible interest. Interest is the largest component of your mortgage payment and offers you a huge tax break when you file your taxes.

On a conventional fixed mortgage, the monthly payment is applied to the principle balance of your loan, which reduces your obligation. The way amortization works, the principle portion of your principle and interest payment increases slightly every month. It is lowest on your first payment and highest on your last payment. On average, each $100,000 of a mortgage will reduce in balance the first year by only about $500 in principal, bringing that balance at the end of your first 12 months to $99,500, but your tax deduction is very high that year because of the amount of interest that you have paid in.

FINAL REVIEW OF THE HOME BUYING PROCESS

As has been stated, buying a home is a very exciting time, but it requires a lot of time, effort, energy, sacrificing and learning the process in order to be an intelligent shopper. Your credit score will play a major role in the process and will determine the rates you will get. If you are knowledgeable, you will know the right questions to ask and will be less likely to be taken advantage of. Once you stick the keys in the door for the very first time, the feeling is one that none can compare to.

You will have achieved the American Dream of Home Ownership. Good luck!

FINANCIAL TIPS TO REMEMBER:

✓ The smartest thing to do in preparation for buying your new home is to pay off as many of your bills as you can and get a copy of your Credit Report.

✓ Unless you shop around for a good mortgage loan, you will almost certainly pay too much in interest rates. This can cost you *tens of thousands of dollars* over the life of your loan, so choose the lowest rate and be wise.

✓ It is wise to get a minimum of two loan estimates and choose the one with the lowest interest rate and ideally no points.

✓ Good credit with high FICO scores means that you will get favorable terms on your loan. Bad credit might prevent you from getting any loan.

✓ Your mortgage payment should not be more than 32% of your gross monthly income. Mortgage payments normally include principal, interest, taxes and insurance also known as P.I.T.I. for short.

✓ Your entire monthly debt load should not be more than 40% of your gross monthly income.

✓ The way amortization works, the principle portion of your principle and interest payment increases slightly every month. It is lowest on your first payment and highest on your last payment.

INDEX/GLOSSARY

Adjustable-rate mortgage (77, 78, 80)
Adjustable-rate Mortgages offer initial rates that are lower than fixed mortgages. At some point, however, usually after the first year, the rates are tied to market conditions and are subject to rate increases. Most ARMs have a cap on rate increases in any given year, as well as over the life of the loan.

Annual Percentage Rate (20, 24, 82, 85, 88, 89, 90)
The interest on credit is usually expressed as an Annual Percentage Rate (APR). The APR usually appears in the "terms" section of the Credit Application and takes into account how long it will take you to pay back the loan.

Appraisal (72, 95)
An appraisal is an estimate of the actual value of the home by a neutral third party at the time you are trying to purchase.

Balloon Payment (86, 105)
While homeowners originally may have had twenty or thirty years to pay on the mortgage, under loan flipping they might be signing for a two, three, or five year balloon payment. At the end of that time they need to find a way to refinance the house again or lose it completely.

Checking Account (2, 37, 73)
A checking account is money that is put into an account that you write checks out of and typically pay bills from.

Savings Account (2, 3, 11, 21, 33, 36, 62, 63)
A savings account is an account that you put money into and typically do not touch, but you allow it to grow by continuing to put money in it. It should only be used in dire emergencies.

Closing Agent (96, 97, 98)
The Closing Agent will inform all relevant parties of the date, time and place of where the closing will be held.

Closing Day (71, 72, 80, 90, 96, 97, 99)
This is the big day, the day that the house officially becomes yours. To close means to "close" the deal on the contract made between you and the seller to buy the home. At closing, the transfer of ownership of the house from the seller to you will officially be made and all monies owed will be paid during this time.

Conventional Mortgage (76, 78, 80, 81, 82, 83, 84, 94, 99)
Fifteen or thirty-year fixed-rate mortgages are considered conventional and are the most popular. The longer the term the lower your monthly payment will be. A fixed rate provides stability over the life of your loan.

Credit (3,4,6,12,17, 18-23, 33, 38-40, 59, 62-64, 67-69, 70,71,73, 74,75,85)
Credit is receiving something without fully paying for it at the time that you get it. It can be defined as faith in your ability and intention to pay for or pay back what has been borrowed or purchased.

Credit Bureaus (18-22, 25, 27, 28)
A Credit Bureau is an agency that gathers information on how consumers use their credit and how they pay back what they borrowed. Credit bureaus collect your information from as many financial transactions or inquiries as they can.

Credit Report (4, 5, 12, 17, 18, 19, 22, 25-28, 59, 61)
Your Credit Report is a detailed record of your payment history with lenders and is an indicator that reflects how well or badly you manage your financial matters.

Discount Points (76, 89)
Closing costs may include loan origination fees and up-front "points" (prepaid interest).

      *For example, if you can afford a maximum monthly payment of $1,000, you will be looking at a total mortgage of $166,792 [assuming a 30-year fixed rate at six percent].

Emergency Fund (2, 8-11, 15, 29, 31, 42, 52)
Like every other recurring item in your budget, the Emergency Fund is something you put money into each month until you reach your desired goal. The purpose of the Emergency Fund is in the case of a job loss. You should have anywhere between 3-6 months salary in this fund.

Escrow Account (96, 103,)
The rationale behind having this account is to protect the lender by ensuring that you pay your taxes and insurance on time. When an Escrow Account is opened, you will keep it throughout the term of your loan. Money put in an escrow account is held by a neutral third party called an Escrow Agent who is someone from a title company or an escrow company.

Federal Housing Association or FHA Loan (48, 63, 64, 68)
The FHA Loan is a partially guaranteed loan which makes it easier for banks to give. Through the FHA Loan, the government guarantees part of your loan to the bank, so if you default, FHA will pay the bank back if you fail to make your payments.

Federal Insurance Contributions Act or FICA Tax (53,57)
FICA tax is a percentage of money that is taken out of the paychecks of working individuals to pay Social Security Retirement and Medicare (Hospital Insurance) benefits to older Americans. It is a mandatory payroll deduction for every working individual.

Federal Withholding (48, 62-64)
This is the biggest income tax that you pay to the federal government which comes directly out of your paycheck. You are required to fill out a W-4 Form when you are hired by a new employer and this determines how much federal withholding will be taken out of your check.

Fixed-rate Mortgages (72, 77-81, 99)
This is a mortgage in which the interest rate does not change during the entire life of the loan.

Going Automatic (2, 6, 7, 11, 49-50)
This means having money automatically taken out of your account for a specific purpose. You don't have to worry about taking the money out yourself. It automatically comes out usually on the day you get paid or the day after. People have automatic withdrawals for things like retirement, emergency fund, savings account, bills, etc.

Good Faith Estimate or GFE (75, 76)
The Good Faith Estimate referred to as a GFE is just that - an estimate and must be provided within three business days of applying for a loan. It is a standard form which is intended to be used to compare different offers from different lenders or brokers.

Gross Debt Service or GDS Ratio (76)
Your mortgage payment should not be more than 32% of your gross monthly income. Mortgage payments normally include principal, interest, taxes and insurance also known as P.I.T.I. for short.

Gross income (53, 63, 72, 76, 100)
The amount of money you make before deductions are taken out.

Home Inspection (72, 95)
An inspector will go through the property and perform a comprehensive visual inspection to assess the condition of the house and all of its systems. He or she will look for hidden problems with the home such as structural, electrical, wiring, water damage, etc.

Interest-only Mortgage. (80, 81)
Only mortgage payments are made up of interest only and do not include any principal. When the loan is due, the original balance is still due.

Lender (13, 17, 63-64, 66-68, 73-74, 76-77, 82-84)
They loan you money for the things you are trying to buy. You must pay this money back with interest. The better your credit is, the less interest you will pay.

Loan flipping (86, 101)
Loan flipping occurs when a *balloon payment* is inserted into the fine print. While the homeowners originally may have had twenty or thirty years to pay on the mortgage, under loan flipping they might be signing for a two, three, or five year balloon payment.

Medicare Tax (48, 63, 68, 103)
Medicare tax is 1.45% and is taken out of your check. Medicare is hospital insurance that benefits older Americans. It is a mandatory payroll deduction for every working individual.

Monthly expenses (11, 12, 13)
This is the amount of money that you spend every month on all the bills in your household, which includes mortgage/rent, car payment, insurance, food, utilities, groceries, credit card payments,

Mortgage Brokers (73-75, 83, 85-88, 93)
Mortgage Brokers are the only ones who *specialize* in the area of finding home loans. Brokers know the market and can be a valuable source of information concerning the home buying process.

Negative-amortization (82, 99, 10)
Negative amortization occurs when the monthly payment is less than full interest and does not pay any principal. The interest that is unpaid accrues and the principle balance owed increases.

Net income (3, 64)
This is the amount of money you bring home each month after all taxes and deductions have come out.

Pre-approval (74, 76, 78)
A pre-approval is means that the lender may commit to giving you a loan if you meet certain requirements and if the home you plan on buying meets certain conditions.

Predatory Lending (75, 82, 83-84, 86-88)
Predatory Lending takes unfair advantage of a homeowner's financial needs by charging unconscionable fees and charges.

Prequalification (72)
A prequalification helps you focus on homes you can afford. A prequalification is when a professional gives you an estimate of how much money you "may" be able to borrow based upon your gross income and amount of debt.

Real Estate Agent (91, 92, 96)
Your Real Estate Agent's job is to provide you with pertinent information about homes for sale and take you out to look at houses. Based on the information you give on the kind of home you want, your Real Estate Agent will search the Multiple

Listing System (MLS) and identify homes that meet your needs and price range.

Spending Plan (9, 35)
This is a budget that you stick to in order to save money. A spending plan helps you to live within or below your means.

Subprime Mortgages (75, 82-85)
Subprime" mortgages carry high fees, high interest rates, strips the borrower of equity in their home and/or places the borrower in a lower credit rating status in order to benefit the subprime lender.

Total Debt Service (TDS) ratio (76)
Your entire monthly debt load should not be more than 40% of your gross monthly income. This includes debts such as car payment(s), credit card payments or other loans.

Veteran Affairs or VA Loans (79)
This type of loan is only offered to veterans and it is not uncommon for them not to put a penny down. As with FHA loans, the VA guarantees part of the loan to the bank if the homeowner defaults, which makes lenders feel comfortable lending the money.

W4 Form (48, 62) A form that is completed when you are hired. This is when you decide how many deductions you will be claiming, which determines how much federal withholding will be taken out.

ABOUT DR. MERRITT

Dr. Mia Y. Merritt was born and raised in South Florida and attended school in the Miami-Dade County Public School System. She is an educator with over 17 years experience working with students as a teacher, Assistant Principal, College Professor and mentor. She is a Certified Keynote Motivational Speaker, Teen/Youth Facilitator, Radio Talk Show Host, Prosperity Coach and Author. She holds a Bachelors Degree in Elementary Education, a Masters Degree in Exceptional Education and a Doctorate Degree in Organizational Leadership with a concentration in Conflict Resolution.

Dr. Merritt is the President/CEO of M&M Motivating, which provides services in corporate retreats, conference speaking, seminars, staff development and teen/youth training. She also writes online articles on various subjects and maintains a Wednesday's Wisdom Blog.

Her Radio Talk Show is on WZAB 880am or www.880thebiz.com every Monday at 11:30am and every Thursday at 4:30pm. The show is called, *The Business of Money*. She and her co-host Ann McNeil discuss ways that money can be made in various areas, industries and fields when people utilize the skills, effort, energy and abilities.

Dr. Mia Y. Merritt
M&M Motivating and Professional Speaking
www.miamerritt.com
1-866-560-7652
merrittmia@yahoo.com

www.ingramcontent.com/pod-product-compliance
Lightning Source LLC
Chambersburg PA
CBHW020918090426
42736CB00008B/688